AND IT TOOK TWO YEARS

SCOTT SPIESS

"In his own words, Scott describes a profound inner healing journey to transformation. He found energy work, Reiki, massage, and mentors that helped him stay on track on his two-year plan to release control and discover his Divine essence. It took a major health challenge and other heavy-duty experiences to ignite a fire for a new beginning. This book is highly recommended to anyone being faced with the challenges of living who has a desire for healing, hope, truth, and enlightenment. I love this book and am very proud of Scott!"
~*Marion Hakata, RMT, CMT, Founder of Living Reiki*

*I dedicate this book to the people who are life-changers.
You in some way, shape, or form have influenced a
life-changing event in another person. I salute you and
humbly thank you for your efforts.*

AND IT TOOK TWO YEARS

FOREWORD

This book called to me for personal reasons. A publisher asked me to write it. I felt some resistance because of ego reasons. I had this inner battle because I did change. I went from a goal-oriented person to someone who today has learned to just let life flow. It is possible to change unwanted or what I call "expired thought" and action patterns. I needed to change for reasons we'll get into later in this book—and it was the right time to make that change. Did it hurt? Yes. Did it really take two years? Yes. Would I do it again? Hell yes! Giving up control or stopping being a control freak turned out to be the most liberating experience I have ever had. It was also one of the hardest things I have ever done. Why would I learn to just let go and see what happens? Simple, the universe and everyone around me told me that I did not need to hyper-control everything. I just needed to listen and get my ego out of the way of organic change and progress.

The more I thought about my two-year journey, the more I decided this story was worth telling—and a story worth reading. I wanted this book to empower everyone who read it to realize that organic change is possible. The primary reason I wrote this book came from my desire to help realize positive change. Everyone has the ability to change. In my example, I went from being a type A, ego-driven, self-centered athlete to someone who became a Buddhist, Reiki Master, and Certified Massage Therapist. I also began volunteering to help others realize their goals. I learned to let go of being a control freak to allow the universe to steer for a while—and you can do it, too.

In the coming pages, I'm going to walk you through my life story and teach you how in just two years I did, in fact, make those changes. I hope by my example, you will see how any change can be made. – *Scott Spiess*

INTRODUCTION

I had a problem on my hands that a lot of people face. I was change-resistant. I felt unwilling to look myself in the mirror and readily go along with change. Learning to change isn't just my problem. I see it on a daily basis in people I know and work with who have the same problem—just a slightly different version. Everyone's story is unique to them, and only they can change their lives for the better. This universal problem is the crux of this book. It begs the question: What does it take to push you over the ledge of change resistance and accept the changes that follow? Not just accept them, but learn to embrace them.

My two-year journey exposed me to many things I did wrong in my life. Wrong is a strong word, but it fits with my old mindset and how I had been acting toward myself and others. I knew that some changes needed to happen, but I did not have the courage to make those changes. It is easier to see fault in others before you see them in yourself.

In the following chapters, I will outline some of the lessons I learned on my journey. I received a lot of painful and positive feedback along the way from others, and that information helped me in the change process. I'm impressed that while going through this two-year process, some pretty awful things happened, but I grew stronger from them. With my newfound skills and attitude, I let those negative things roll off my back.

Sometimes you become aware of issues that you did not know you had; however, it is how you deal with those problems that matters. I learned to let things go by seeing the bigger picture in life and finally reaching the conclusion that I could accept necessary changes. I felt empowered once I made a decision to no longer look to the past for answers. The answers were in front of me, and I needed to roll forward and let the organic change happen. I hope my story teaches others how to positively move forward in their lives, too. As I learned, it's well worth the effort to achieve the amazing outcome: a life lived with peace of mind, happiness, and gratitude.

THE OLD ME

To understand where I was in life you need to know the old me. To see a picture of my past life is to think big, act big, and follow through with your commitments. This all sounds great and is what you should do, but it's just not healthy to always swing for the fence. The following quote by T. E. Lawrence pretty much sums up my mindset at the time. Through passion and unstoppable drive, I dared to dream during the day and then acted on it.

"All men dream, but not equally. Those who dream by night in the dusty recesses of their minds, wake in the day to find that it was vanity: but the dreamers of the day are dangerous men, for they may act on their dreams with open eyes, to make them possible."
- T. E. Lawrence

I am one who dreams during the day and acts on those dreams. I used to have a saying that I lived by—call it my motto: *"I think, therefore I do."* It means I can and will do anything I put my mind toward accomplishing. It does not make a difference if this "something" takes a little time to accomplish or even years. Achieving a goal at any price *became* the goal, and failure wasn't an option. This mindset, of course, doesn't mean I would steamroll over other people to achieve the goal. It meant I competed with other people to obtain the goal in the fairness of competition.

Anyone can win on any day if they play their cards right. This outlook made me a bit of a simple person to understand. I am driven and can be considered a person focused on his or his team's goals. I most valued what I could do compared to others in the realm of competition. This is how I measured myself and assigned worth to my life. It's not an easy way to live your life. You're constantly competing with the world around you and having to live up to a very high standard. I was raised this way— and I apologize to no one for it. I am immensely proud of what I have been able to accomplish. I had earned a position on the US National Cycling team and been a rock climber, runner, skydiver, triathlete, motorcycle racer, white-water kayaker, cross-country skiing racer, and a 24-hour endurance car racer. How I saw the world was through *doing* things others only dreamed about doing and succeeding at them—that was the *old* me.

AND IT BEGINS

It was 2016, and I looked forward to the year ahead. The last three years had been really challenging by anyone's standards. Diagnosed with an aortic aneurysm, I faced the end of my competitive athletic career. It had taken its toll on me. I had been hit hard physically and emotionally. I felt so tired of dealing with it. I officially felt sorry for myself, and I did not have a standard to live by anymore. Competition as a way of life had gone out the window. I faced a rocking chair on the front porch, which now called to me by name. What I most valued had gone up in smoke, and only vapor trails got left behind.

How this happened goes like this ... one day I went into the doctor's office to have my physical for my Sports Car Club of America (SCCA) racecar driver's license and the next thing I knew I failed my physical. How could this be? Just a few months earlier I ran a local running race the 3rd Annual Gems 5K in my home town of Lincoln, Ca. Not my distance of choice, but at age 47 I ran an 18:10. That is 5:51 per mile. I won my age division, and I was fifth overall. I saw this as a huge win and a success for my running coach Dan, a manager at the local running store. How can someone who is running sub six-minute miles fail a physical? It is called stage two hypertension. There is something bad about having a blood pressure of 160 over 90. Yes, that is high, and the doctors prescribed a long list of blood pressure drugs to combat it. Along with those terrible drugs, I also got set up for all kinds of tests and scans to participate in. The doctors wanted to see if there was anything else wrong with me.

There was a really good reason to go on a fishing expedition with the scans—they found an aortic aneurysm on my heart. The scans confirmed the diagnosis and searched for more aneurysms. The doctors stressed if they found one on my aorta then there were probably more of them. So, an upper and lower cat scan got ordered with contrast dye. I honestly did not want the scans, but the doctors saw them as medically necessary. I just felt the further I went along with this exploration, the worse it would get for me. I would rather die fighting than bend a knee in surrender to all of these doctors telling me that the sedate lifestyle now headed my direction. The cat scans found and measured my aortic aneurysm but did not find any other abnormalities. I should have been happy with the news but I was not. I felt terrified about the changes in my life that were about to become my new reality.

My athletic career had ended—and I did not want to admit it. The cat scans also found two nodules in my lungs that measured 5MM each. This caught the eye of my cardiologist. I was in trouble. I didn't want to contemplate what might come next. I kept feeling like my life as I knew it had just ended. Now the only place I would be comfortable would be in a rocking chair on the porch. This news put me on my ass, and I didn't get up fast. I honestly never liked rocking chairs since as a kid I had broken by big toe on one.

The new reality included beta-blockers prescribed by my doctor to slow the contractions of my heart—and by my estimation these pills took 30 percent of my heart's blood-pumping ability away from me. The doctors also prescribe this solution since theoretically if they took away my ability to do harm to myself by running or another activity, I would not be able to do more damage to my heart and the aneurysm wouldn't grow.

There is a downside to all this, and I didn't feel very happy about it. I used to be able to run a 6:30-mile training pace—and I could run a half-marathon at that pace. Now I could barely run an 8-minute-mile and even that required working really hard at it.

I felt seriously depressed about this situation, and I did not know what to do. I wanted to workout but it simply was no fun anymore. The doctors could not tell me how my aneurysm happened or when it happened—and that too caused a lot of frustration and anger. If it happened a long time ago when I raced bikes, and it had not grown since then, I would be in the clear. If it had recently grown, I was in trouble with it expanding. I would need to have a heart operation to the fix the problem. At that time, I planned everything and didn't easily go with the flow. I needed answers to my questions. The doctors just stared at me in amazement that I would dare ask the question and not let them say, "I do not know." "I do not know" is not an acceptable response and left me in limbo. I still wanted my old life back, and I wanted to compete again. I participated in my own version of "You cannot fix stupid." I panicked because my whole life had been based on competition. So now I went into flight or fight mode.

I started lashing out at people, which made me no fun to be around. I told my doctor, who found my high blood pressure and ordered the scans, that she ruined my life to save my life. I told her that I wished she had never found it. I told her I would rather die fighting than surrender to all of the medications. The side effects sucked, as I could not do anything I used to do with ease. I should not be out of breath mowing the lawn let alone climbing some stairs. I had to work so much harder than before. I did not care that my statement hurt the doctor's feelings. I felt pissed off and in a state where I could not calm myself down. I ended up in a very dark place, and I have been in dark places before.

My current situation was different than anything I had been exposed to. Before I still had options to pick up another sport and go for it. I would "rinse and repeat" if I still felt terrible. Feeling hurt, I felt mad at the world. Put another way, "hurt people hurt people." This put me in an emotional limbo that I would not wish on anyone.

The doctors happily told me that my aneurysm wasn't large enough to do anything about, so we went into a "watch-and-wait" mode. I didn't like the watch-and-wait mode. I am a person of action. I had no issue making a decision to fix myself. I wanted to be fixed. My doctors told me that I looked at my situation all wrong. This really frustrated me because I just wanted to be fixed, and I am not risk-adverse. I figured a smaller aneurysm should be easier to fix, so let's get to it.

To pile onto this already messed-up situation, my cardiologist called me on the evening of December 24th at around 5 PM to tell me I had lung cancer. I was floored. What the hell? My wife was born on December 24, and I just ruined her birthday night. I know cancer is more important than a birthday, it just did not help the situation. My wife always hated her birthday because it was on Christmas Eve and to add a cancer diagnosis attached to her birthday made her unhappy. Lung cancer is not a present worth giving.

At the time I did not think about the scope of practice of my cardiologist. I was in shock. I thought the end was coming. I do not want to ride the crazy train to my death. My anxiety had nothing to do with death itself. I have always been fine with thinking about my own death. I am just weird that way. My cardiologist did not remember his scope of practice by giving me the cancer news. The cardiologist had no idea about lung cancer as pulmonary, and it's not in his wheelhouse. He had no qualifications to make a cancer diagnosis. My cardiologist ended up having to talk with a pulmonary doctor, and the pulmonary doctor handed him his head.

The pulmonary doctor clearly explained the scanning technologies are so much better now, that formations in the lungs showing up in cat scans isn't always cancer. You cannot just call the nodules cancer, and in doing so my cardiologist had an ego the size of Mt. Everest. You are responsible for your actions one way or another. In his mind, he simply could not do anything wrong, nor admit that he had been wrong. A week or so later my cardiologist retracted his diagnosis and blamed it on scanning technology during an office visit. He told me to forget about it, and we needed to move on. I could not fire that doctor fast enough. Since he diagnosed me with lung cancer, and it was now in my medical records, I would now have to endure two years of cat scans—all because of his error that was considered resolved.

After this point, I decided that I would never take a doctor's findings as the final answer. I would question everything. Doctors are people, and sometimes people make mistakes. Doctors are no exception to the rule, and sometimes they reach a conclusion too quickly. Since I work for a hospital, I see this all the time—and time and time again, they are wrong. I will state this several times in this book. I never respect those who cannot admit that they make mistakes. I'll say it again, *you are responsible for your actions one way or another*. Not being able to admit he made a mistake just made himself look weak and petty in my eyes.

Since that experience, when it comes to medical care, I am now my best health advocate. I never allowed that cardiologist to treat me again, and I sure as hell will never recommend him to anyone. By the way, I do not have lung cancer, as the two areas have not increased in size after two-years plus of scans. My pulmonary doctor has come to the same conclusion. This is yet another reason that I will always advocate for myself over doctor's findings: double fail on the diagnosis of lung cancer and not being able to admit he was wrong.

With this news of cancer and my aortic aneurysm, I spiraled down into an even darker hole. I started to spend a lot of time reflecting on my past accomplishments and disappointments and how many times I seemed to get the shaft on things. I felt sorry for myself. In reality, I had no right to feel sorry for myself, because I actually have lived an extraordinary life thus far. I needed to take the good with the bad and make something out of it. Does anyone have some lemons? I have been able to do things that people only dream about, and all I saw was that I could not get back to my old self. I wasn't content with where I was at that moment. My daydreaming needed to take a rest—or so I thought.

Some of my past accomplishments included representing my country in the Jr. World Championships in Mery Corbon, France in 1984. I spent two years on the US National Cycling Team, and I represented our country in foreign lands. I have been to Egypt, Israel, Turkey, and Greece. I have free-solo rock climbed while being afraid of heights. I have skydived over 100 times, and I have hung from the plane's wing upside down while doing it. I have whitewater kayaked in the state of Veracruz in southern Mexico. I never let a challenge beat me, and I was always up for the next one.

The downside to all this excitement and bravado is that the higher you fly the farther you fall—and that fall comes fast and deep. I did not like what I had become. I have never been good at being a lost soul and feeling sorry for myself. I have been depressed before and once took a run at suicide. I take that back. I did not complete that task. I am a "suicidal failure," and I am damn proud of it. The ending of my cycling career had been really hard on me. I would watch the Tour de France and see my friends racing. For a while, I could not watch any bike racing—it ripped open old wounds. My current situation made me feel trapped, and I had a limited list of options—or so I thought. Perspective is a funny thing. Just when you think there are no other options, a door opens and if you are brave enough to accept the challenge, there is more life out there to live.

When I get this way, I used to let my brain slide into the most significant moment of my life. This event had been the start and peak of my ability and allowed me to dream big. Just like the T.S. Lawrence quote at the beginning of the book, I am a daydreamer—and I dare to put those dreams into action. It isn't healthy or right to look to your past for your dreams. I have a habit of doing this when I have nowhere else to go. It's a special place in my head. I do have a good case of living in the past with significant moments that give me positive memories and emotionally charged feelings. I always considered this to be normal, but I soon found out it wasn't healthy.

My most significant moment is not getting married; it is not the birth of a child; it is winning my first bike race. The race took place in 1984 at the Camellia Festival Criterium, an annual bike race in February. The weather had been terrible that year.

It rained a lot and had been very cold. The Camellia Festival Criterium, the first race of the year, found me ready to go. I won by jumping the field with 400 yards to go. I held off the field due to special off-season training. The special training was pretty old school for the time. No, I did not use performance-enhancing drugs like Lance Armstrong. I did not use some sort of new cycling technology either. I did not use steroids, which was pretty obvious. I was a super scrawny, little teenager. I weighed in at about 137 pounds at the time. I used hard work and determination. How about that? Work hard and play hard. The special training involved roller racing. Rollers, a training aid, help you ride smoothly. You can work on your leg speed. Rollers help smooth out your pedal stroke and your turnover or revolution rate, which was my secret weapon. No one trains to sprint for 500 yards, but I did.

What happened during the race was pretty simple. I had the confidence that I could sprint in my maximum gear for 500 yards. Now, most bike racing field sprints are around 200-yards long, which is a big gap in distance. As a junior cyclist, I was limited in how high of a gear I could use. This approach gave me an advantage. I could sprint in my maximum gear longer than anyone else that day. I won and that changed my life forever. Most people never get to experience the thrill of accomplishing something like that—and I realized my life would never be the same moving forward.

I still feel the emotional rush of crossing the finishing line, and I still get goosebumps. I am the person I am because of that moment. Winning had been what I wanted to do. It had been perfectly timed. My cycling coach felt so proud of me. His hard work showed that he could take a screwed-up kid and turn that same screwed-up kid into a US National Cycling team member. At the same time, I found my voice and a way of dealing with the world.

THE PHONE RANG

The phone rang and pulled me quickly out of my daydream. My very close friend Mark, who was recently diagnosed with liver cancer, had not been doing well. Andre, my good friend, told me that Mark had passed on and cancer won. Mark had been suffering from stage 4 liver cancer and now his battle had ended. His first round of chemotherapy had killed him. The news sucked all the wind out of me, made me sit down, and put my head between my legs. I really miss Mark—and to this day I think he will walk through the door like nothing ever happened. I cannot watch a Formula One car race without thinking about him and what he meant to me.

I felt devastated for Mark's family and myself. I didn't want to face that Mark died and would never come back. At that moment frustration and anger hit me like a freight train. I had known that I wanted to make some changes in my life for a while, and Mark's death was the straw that broke my will of resistance to change. I didn't like where my personal life had gone, because of all my health issues. I needed to find a way to change without looking to the past for solutions. Game on.

MARK

Every journey has its start with the first step, and my journey would not be any different. I have experienced many life-changing events, but Mark's death broke my will of resistance to change. I had been resistant to change because I knew that it would hurt to open up all the old wounds. It is not like I had a ton of terrible events in my life, but this one just hit me pretty hard.

Mark, a happy-go-lucky, 60-plus-year-old guy who everyone just adored, entered a room and his personality lit up the room. He was friends with everyone. Mark was the kind of guy who collected lost souls and became the glue that kept them all together.

Mark and I had several passions in common, and cars were one of them. Mark first encountered me when he saw me pull my sports car out of my neighborhood. He stood in his upstairs back bedroom and looked out the window when he saw me. He said, "Oh my God, that is a Lotus Super 7." In reality, it is a Birkin S3 Roadster made in South Africa, but it is the same design that Colin Chapman designed for Lotus. I had gone out on a Sunday drive in a speedy kind of way when he saw me. This chance sighting became the foundation of a soon-to-be-friendship. I have always found it amazing just how connected things are once a "chance" encounter turns into so much more. I have learned a lot over the two years of this journey, and one important lesson is that everything is connected. Nothing happens in a vacuum.

The following Monday I received a phone call from John, one of my freelance computer customers. I was a technology instructor for a national private college, which was my day job, and I needed some extra money. I had set up a side business doing computer jobs to augment my income and keep my hands active with current technology.

John owns a small accounting firm, and he notoriously took the less expensive option every opportunity he could. I constantly battled with him over long-term solutions versus short-term bandaids. Bandaid solutions always cost you more in the long run. We had several projects that were successful in the beginning but broke after six months of use. John's company moved into a new office space. He wanted to know how he could lower my bill. Since I just wanted to do the server work, I suggested that he find a PC tech to help him out. John had an obsession about the cost and not about what I could do to automate his accounting firm.

At the time, Mark worked at an office supply store as an entry-level PC tech. Just starting out in the computer field, Mark found this office store did pretty good business. Mark enjoyed working at the office store since everyone loved his personality and his work ethic. This allowed Mark to learn about technology in a controlled environment without the risks of doing installations at people's homes or businesses.

John found Mark through a friend. He felt excited because Mark charged one-third of what I charged. John gave Mark my phone number to call to see if Mark could do the whole computer computer system move. Mark called me that evening. He tried to feel me out about John. Mark asked if I really told John to find a PC tech to do the PC work? I said yes I did and let Mark know that I wasn't really interested in the PC work. "So, you're helping John out by doing that work." Mark got energized and kept asking more and more detailed questions about the company move.

Mark finally asked the question that I knew John had put him up to doing. "What are the chances that I can do all the work?" Mark acted super nice on the phone, and he asked in the right way. I told Mark that if he could answer my questions, then he had enough skill to do the company move by himself. I asked, if he was familiar with Microsoft Small Business Edition Server? I also asked him if he had the IP address information for the external interface on the company's firewall? I started into a couple of other questions around DNS (Domain Name Service), and Mark jumped in and said, "I have no clue what you are saying." I followed up with him and said, "Then it's good we are having this conversation." I then asked him how I could help him be successful with this customer—and we came up with a plan.

Mark really wanted to work with the accounting company, as this was his first external computer customer outside the office supply company. Mark would transport all the PCs to the new location and cable them all up, and I would transport the server to the new office. Then I would reconfigure the firewall with the new IP addresses and make sure all the networking worked. I would get the server up and running and ensure all the PCs connected with the server shares. I told Mark that we could do it pretty quickly if we were organized—and on move day it went off without a problem.

We formed a friendship that day that would last quite a few years. During the accounting firm's move Mark and I talked about cars, computers, and wives. At this time, he figured out I was the guy driving the Lotus. I corrected him that it was a Birkin, but to Mark, it really didn't matter, he just looked at me and said, "Cool car."

REIKI, I WANTED TO HELP

After Mark's cancer diagnosis, I really wanted to do something to help him. He had been a close friend for more than five years, so I naturally put in the effort for him. I also needed to make sense of what was happening to him. Cancer is a serious matter. I knew the odds were not in his favor. I didn't know what to do for him, but I needed to do *something*.

I'm a plan-and-execute type of guy. I come up with a plan first, then I execute it, and I know the outcome. When you just have to do something without thinking or planning it, what you get are unintended consequences. These unintended consequences usually turn out to be worse than the problem you want to fix. Without reason or intention, these activities usually go awry. You try to engineer an outcome without knowing what you engineer it for. For example, has a politician ever actually solved a problem, or did he/she make it worse through their efforts? This makes them the problem, not the solution. So to combat any lack of ideas I did what any computer guy would do—I hit the Internet. I searched for a remedy for cancer side effects. I wanted to do something that was personal and worked to support him in his time of need.

I found something called Reiki, which is an energy modality in massage. Some massage therapists do not like to admit that, but it is. Energy work or light work is part of massage therapy, and it subscribes to the mantra of "do no harm." Reiki has five key precepts or a daily oath to align you to good intentions and to be a good person.

Today only

Do not anger

Do not worry

With thankfulness

Work diligently (at Reiki)

Be kind to others

To understand Reiki you must know that all bodies have an energy field. This is not a surprise to most people, but within those bodies, there are areas that are stronger with energy than others. For the sake of argument, let us call those areas "energy centers". These energy centers vary with energy, and the idea is to balance out the energy field and energy centers to promote proper energy flow and emotional well being. I am oversimplifying my description of Reiki and how you use it a bit for demonstrative purposes, but a basic understanding is needed.

You also have situations where you find what I refer to as "stale energy" areas. These stale areas feel gummy or slightly sluggish to me and might feel different for others. Through the process of using several different hand positions, you can balance the energy in the body and remove the stale energy. I like to refer to Reiki as my energy body just saying hello to your energy body, with balancing as the desired outcome. You act as a conduit for the energy to flow through you.

Reiki isn't scary. It's a little woo-woo to talk about it, but I am fine with that. Reiki isn't a cure and should never be considered a cure. Reiki assists the body to heal itself through balancing of energy. Reiki is also not a religion. There is no deity or faith in Reiki.

So with my newfound knowledge on Reiki, I felt ready to give it a try. I took an uncharted leap into Reiki to be surprised by what I found. I wanted to try Reiki to help Mark, as I felt it would work. Mark had trouble with headaches. I figured that Reiki could be the solution for the pain. I thought Reiki's calming nature would help. Reiki has a way of dissipating stress and anxiety.

To learn how to use Reiki, I found a lot of options, but the majority of the options took too long to accomplish. I needed to act quickly and find some training around Reiki. Thus, I could not go the traditional route, which requires you to work in person with a Reiki Master. Finding a Reiki Master is not a problem, but working with him or her is another issue—and for me a very big issue. I had several discussions with Reiki Masters. They had a lot of extra rules on training time and how many practice sessions I needed to do before I could take the next class. I felt that would be a burden and take too much time. I needed to help Mark now. Taking a year to get my training wasn't going to happen. The question became, "Where would I get my Reiki training?" I soon found an online education and entertainment website that had Reiki training on it. The online classes were not expensive, and you can take them at your own pace.

I signed up for Reiki training from beginning through master. I quickly crammed six-plus hours of videos and read a 250-page book. I avoided the attunement section of the course. Attunements allow the Reiki Master or teacher of Reiki to initiate their students to the different Reiki symbols. You could consider this a rite-of-passage ceremony. I do have a future plan that if I stick with Reiki, I will go back to Reiki training in the traditional manner. I thought this was a fair trade-off since I wasn't representing myself as something I am not in the Reiki community.

I finished my Reiki training. Now I felt ready to help Mark. I spent more than 40 hours digging through the training videos and the Reiki book. The book ended up being the best thing about the class. Yes, the videos were nicely put together and informative, but the book allowed me to quickly go back to a subject. I found searching a video far more time consuming. You had to search through a long video, and you did not always know which video had the information.

Now I let Mark know I wanted to help him—and he surprised me with his answer. Mark was not receptive to Reiki—he thought it was a strange idea. I couldn't fault him for his lack of knowledge about Reiki. I didn't know what Reiki was before I started training either. I hadn't checked with him before starting Reiki training. He looked at it like a religion. There goes my unintended consequence. Ok, so much for proper communications, planning, and execution.

Mark was a born-again Christian. In his state of being close to death, he did not want to do anything that would jeopardize his faith. I explained I was available to help him when he felt ready. He wanted to first check with his spiritual advisor. I, of course, agreed to wait, especially since I took his opinion very seriously on the matter. You can work remotely with Reiki, but you need to get permission before you do remote work. The person receiving Reiki must agree to be part of the process. You never use Reiki on an unwilling person, as it is disrespectful.

It took two weeks from the time I told him I could help him using Reiki before he agreed to receive Reiki. I honestly got a little concerned because I thought that I went through all this effort and wouldn't be able to help him. I then had a self-realization and said to myself, "Stop being an ass, it is not about you! Mark is dying." I needed to get my ego out of the way. I thought, "*So what if I spent all this time learning a new skill. You did it for a friend and that is it.*" If Mark did not want my help using Reiki, it was his decision and only his decision.

Mark's spiritual advisor told him that there was nothing wrong with Reiki. It wasn't a religion. Upon hanging up the phone I went over to his house right away. Mark and I had talked on the phone many times during his sickness, but I was taken aback by what I saw when I arrived at his house. I, of course, hid my feelings since I was there to help him. Unneeded emotion weren't going to be helpful at this point. I just needed to pretend to be British and show my stiff upper lip.

I know Mark felt self-conscious about his current state. Mark rested upstairs in the master bedroom because it was comfortable for him, and he had everything he needed up there. Mark retained a lot of water and his belly had become quite bloated. I greeted him in our usual warm manner. He told me how much he hated having all this extra weight. The extra weight caused him to not sleep well. He felt uncomfortable in any position except sitting. I stayed very present with Mark and let him talk as much as he wanted to before I went to work on him.

Mark did have some questions about Reiki. He felt confused about what to do as I worked on him. I gave him some simple directions about clearing his mind and to sit with as much laxity as possible. I know he felt terrible with all the water retention, so I kept it really simple and did not go into the relaxation of the body. Simple is good in this type of situation. I explained I was going to have my hands on him in a few locations. He might experience a warming feeling in those locations.

Mark had a raging headache that he could not shake, so that is where I started to work first. Mark being the first person I worked on with Reiki (besides myself), I decided to follow the steps that I had learned in my online class. I said the name of the first two Reiki symbols. I positioned my tongue correctly on the roof of my mouth. I breathed with my lower abdomen in slow, deep, and methodical breaths. I visualized my energy coming from above me heading down my spine to my sacrum and then out of my hands. My hands went instantly hot, which didn't surprise me, and Mark commented that it felt like I had gone into his head. Mark sensed a slight pressure change in his head too. He told me that he felt a nice, warming sensation.

I spent three minutes at each energy center that I could reach. I did some sweeping with my hands to finalize the Reiki session. I instructed Mark to open up his eyes. He said that his headache had gone, and that felt very strange, but it was an amazing experience. I worked on Mark a couple of times before he went into what I called "quarantine mode". Mark had gotten worse, and only close family members were allowed to be with him. Outside people could expose him to foreign agents that might make him even sicker—and no one wanted that.

I asked Mark by way of phone if I could work remotely with Reiki and he accepted. Mark considered the remote Reiki to be a little "whack-a-doodle" but he accepted anyway. He acted like a good sport about all of this. When I worked on Mark remotely I took a picture of him and placed it on my leg. I then visualized his body on the top of my leg and used my Reiki symbols to get started. Working remotely, you tend to move quicker than if you are there with the person.

Mark passed away a few days later, with his family by his side.

I fully appreciate my time with Mark. I considered him a close friend. I don't really have a lot of close friends—and this is why I think losing him to cancer caused me to take a look at my life. I began to understand we are only here for a short period of time. I realized I needed to make my life more meaningful.

TIME TO MAKE SOME CHANGES

A couple of days after Mark's death, I got serious about making some life changes. Up until that point, I had been giving the idea nothing but lip service. I now considered myself a little broken. I didn't know what changes to make. I felt unsure of what to do or how to do it. Do I want to force changes as a plan of attack or do I want those changes to organically happen over time? The idea of change seemed much harder than it should be. Uncertainty led to confusion, which then made me angry at myself and those around me.

It wasn't right to take my frustration and anger out on anyone other than myself. I became careful to check myself if I got too hot under the collar with anyone. I quickly realized my personal frustration of not knowing what to do about changing should not be offloaded on others. I felt that I should be able to figure this out on my own—I am a grown man for god sakes. Remember, I am a planner. So I thought I should be able to plan my changes, but my confusion over the whole thing made that impossible.

The answer came to me about a month later. Out of the blue, I realized that I should not plan anything. I had an epiphany which started the process of letting go. I needed to stop trying to control everything, a totally foreign idea to me.

My family brought me up to plan everything. My father, a civil engineer, had a list for everything with a time and date attached to it. He even planned yard work on the first Saturday of the month. Trimming all the bushes in our yard put everyone on deck to get it done. We had our assigned tasks. The house always looked great, but it was a lot of work. The constant work ruined me to do my own yard work when I grew up.

So, the "anti-plan" had been hatched. Now I would just let things happen organically. The universe needed to steer for a while. The hard parameters I put on my journey required it be completed in two years and any activity would be done with new people. I chose two years to give me enough time to work on things, but not have it be open-ended. I did not want to take so long that it could fade away. This way the universe could have its say, while I would had the ability to take back the decision-making process at the end of the journey.

In the end, I could reflect on what I had learned along the way and have some sort of timetable to work with. I needed a foundational cornerstone to stand on, and the time limit was it. Now anything could happen. I could try new things within that two-year period—all without any negative feelings or thinking I had wasted my time.

In the past trying new things had never been an issue. I used to challenge myself by working on things like fear of heights, fear of drowning, and fear of speed. In some ways, this is a sick joke that I played with myself. I am just wired that way.

I have always had a fear of heights, and it has held me back in some ways; but to combat it, I took up rock climbing and later skydiving. I had a fear of drowning even though I played water polo in high school and swam for the Sacramento City College swim team. I swam the 500, 1000, and 1650 freestyle races as a walk-on swimmer. Then I took up white-water kayaking and used those swimming skills in my "out-of-boat excursions".

The white-water kayaking did get a little out of hand. I took a trip to the state of Veracruz in Mexico to go down free-running rivers right after a hurricane had come through. Those rivers were much bigger white water than I have ever run and more dangerous than I expected. I used my brain and commitment to combat the fear. One really bad day, I helped out in the support raft. Even I knew I had gotten in over my head, and I did not want to be a meme for "You cannot fix stupid." Also, where we were at, there were no hospitals. If I got hurt game over. I had seen friends get hurt fixing their "stupid", and I learned from their mistakes.

I also wanted to overcome my fear of speed. I was never a great downhill cyclist. I could just hold my own in a race or in a heated training ride. I could time-trial and hill-climb like a banshee, but I cautiously road the downhills. To combat that fear I started racing street motorcycles and later became a 24-hour endurance racecar driver. The motorcycle racing cured me of my fear of speed. There is something thrilling about being under semi-control with the bike leaned all the way over with the front and back of the bike sliding. I learned through intensity and honestly loving the rush. I simply could not get enough of it. The bike used to look all out of shape, but I fluidly made it through the corners. My race bike got stolen after my American Federation of Motorcycles (AFM) license qualifier. That ended my motorcycle obsession. Can someone say theft insurance? However, once I conquered my fear of speed, I could not get enough.

I had a couple of directions I could go after my motorcycle racing. I could do car-sprint races or endurance car racing. In sprint racing, you race for 20 minutes. In endurance racing, you race for one and a half hours per stint. I like endurance stints because I drained the car's gas tank and got more seat time. I really enjoyed racing for better than an hour and a half because I lost myself in what I did. In some ways, it felt very surreal. I found it inspirational to be driving as the sun came up. I equate this to a religious experience because it aroused a raw emotional power while I did it.

I remember at the racetrack in Button Willow, Ca. I drove the car as the sun rose. I found myself crying while I drove—it looked so beautiful. I had the ability, like when I trained for bike racing, not to focus on the ordinary but pay attention to the extraordinary. In my case, I wasn't the fastest driver on the track. I drove almost as fast but brought home a healthy car at the end of my stint. This skill also helped keep all my teammates happy. No one likes working on a car at the racetrack that has a blown engine or you have shunted (crashed).

I felt some honor from racing endurance races. One 24-hour car race landed me, and everyone else at Thunder Hill Raceway that day, in the *Guinness Book of World Records*. We won the record for the most cars and drivers at a 24-hour endurance race. We had 216 cars and better than 1,100 drivers. New things with new people are a good thing—and I got to be a part of it. I never dreamed that I would be in the *Guinness Book of World Records*. I used to buy the record books when I was a little kid. The universe is an amazing place when you let go a little.

So, I tried new things with new people and ideas, but how about my ideas? I spent years studying philosophy. I had no problem with critical thinking. Since I have a strong personality and a whole lot of drive, I decided that my ideas needed to take a backseat to other people's ideas. I wanted to really get to know new people I met at events or on the street. You cannot get to know someone by talking to them or talking at them. You need to listen and get to know them through their thoughts about how the world works. You also need to be present with them and meet them on their playing field of perspectives and ideas. I needed to listen first and then speak when spoken to. This is so not me, but it made sense in the end. I wanted people to feel comfortable to open up to me without fear of my quick wit or some questioning reply. Challenging someone when you just meet them is not a good way of getting to know and understand them.

While I was meeting all these new people at events and on the street it became obvious that I needed to seek professional help. I decided that I wanted to find someone to talk to about what

I had been going through and my feelings about it. I wanted someone who had lived a little life and would be willing to get in the trenches with me. I have never been shy about saying what is on my mind or admitting I need help. I have never seen the wisdom of being in physical or emotional pain and not trying to help yourself out of it. When you are sick, you go see a doctor. I needed someone who would challenge me and not put up with my hiding information or avoiding honesty about my problems. I soon found this person by accident … or maybe not!

A word about picking a therapist. Just any old therapist won't necessarily work for you. You become very intimate with your therapist. You should pick a therapist like you would pick a mate. You don't just date them. You need to feel safe with them and have their focus be the same one as yours. You really need to trust this person or you won't get what you need out of the therapist-patient relationship. Never settle for just anyone. Odds are you will not click, and if you want release from your issues, you need that click.

I had been looking around at different social events as a way to get out there and meet people when I stumbled onto The Holistic Lighthouse. One day while playing my obsessively addicting cell phone game called Ingress, I walked into the Holistic Lighthouse. The area around the Lighthouse is a hot zone for Ingress players.

For those that do not know Ingress; Ingress is a game like capture the flag with teams and geo-locations called portals. There are several portals around the Lighthouse. I played outside and became interested in what happened inside the Lighthouse building. When I walked into the Lighthouse I noticed in the lobby there were all kinds of meeting flyers for different events. They also had a whiteboard in the lobby and someone named Samantha posted an event called "The Law of Attraction". The event was free, and I had the night open, so I signed up.

SAMANTHA

I attended Samantha's Law of Attraction event the following Thursday in late December 2016. Halfway through her discussion, I concluded I wanted to work with her. I found Samantha to be a very outspoken but fair person who had some interesting ideas about how the universe works. I attentively listened to her discussing the winding and unwinding of emotional issues and how the body stores those issues. I liked her out-of-the-box thinking, and she impressed me with her candor.

Since I needed to find someone who would have no issue taking me to task when I wavered or tried to avoid the issue, I approached Samantha to help me. Samantha became the 12-pound sledgehammer to the side of my head. She offered the solution for my first round of therapy.

Samantha, a 40-something, tall female, has lived some life. Samantha has long, brownish hair, clear eyes, and a pleasant smile. These attributes help her break the ice with people. Don't let her fool you. Avoid honesty and she can take your head off. I mean this in a positive way. I needed some tough love—and I wasn't above being roughed up a bit. To get to my goal of quieting my mind and living a more attuned life, I had to drop all the walls around me and accept change. My enemy now became resistance to change.

Samantha had a tough life growing up. She is open about being physically abused by her father as a young girl. She admits to an old drug abuse problem. She also confessed she worked as a bartender and dated her customers. What could I possibly say to shock Samantha? Thus, she became the perfect person to go deep—and believe me we did go there. Our calm-but-brutal conversations enabled me to get to the root of my emotional problems.

Now I use the word "therapist" to describe what I did with Samantha, but that is not how I saw Samantha. I used the term therapist/therapy, but she acted more like a soundboard to help me figure things out and pull out the answers. Well, she didn't really "pull" anything. She more like "mass donated" a thermonuclear device—and fallout got everywhere. Once I started letting things out in the open, I also felt like I lost some control. Issues started dripping out like a trickle of water and then gushed like Niagara Falls. The change happened, and I let it out without restrictions. Now I started to win over resistance to change.

At the time, Samantha wanted the first meeting with her to be a 90-minute session. She explained her process and got a feel for the person sitting across from her in therapy. We had met at the Law Attraction event yet it didn't offer a comfortable setting. The 90-minute session in a quiet room allowed Samantha to decide if I was serious about change; otherwise she would decline to work with me.

Samantha, an action-based person, didn't go for indecision. Puttering around about whether I should do something or not just draws change out too long. I am not saying she is not patient; I am saying you need to stay committed to your end goal and work through her process. The process is important. Everyone who follows the process experiences positive results.

In our first cordial session, we engaged in a lot of small talk where she strategically asked questions. I caught onto the questioning pretty early on in the conversation. I went with it. We set up the next session with the goal of covering the requirements that I needed to accomplish and a follow-up discussion on Samantha's process.

A week later, we met for the second session. Samantha had a plan of attack right from the start. The first part of her process required I write letters to people who had hurt me and address that hurt. I remember telling myself that this does not sound so bad and seemed pretty simple. You write a few blurbs about a person who hurt you and tell them how he/she hurt you. I thought, *"I can do that."*

Samantha, right from the starting gate, warned me that I would have to write the letters one at a time and read them out loud during our session. She also warned me to not take this assignment lightly—and I assured her that I would not.

Samantha did something that surprised me at the end of our session. She told me that she did not want to see me until I had done my first letter. She also said the letter had to be heartfelt or she would make me write it over again. I certainly did not want to do it twice. At the time, I flashed back to my early school days and kind of felt like she had scolded me like one of my teachers. However, she imposed this idea to add a little pressure to get the letters done.

I did delay writing the letters. I immediately got stuck. I didn't want to relive the hurt nor put those same feelings on paper. However, I had agreed to this requirement so I had no other choice but to get them done. Just because my therapist wanted something done her way didn't mean I would walk away. After all, I had come to her for help. If writing letters helped then more power to her technique—and to me getting results, right?

That day, I left the session feeling pretty good and motivated to move things forward. I figured that it would take a day or so to write one of the letters. I sat down a couple of days later with the intention to write my first letter yet I couldn't start it. I felt immediately confused like I chased my tail. I didn't have writer's block per se. I already had the content. I just did not know how to say it. I needed a starting point—but I couldn't find anything to give me traction.

This reminded me of an early problem when I encountered Algebra. I wasn't born with the math gene. I remember as a kid getting really upset with an algebra problem. I would yell, "How can I do this math problem when I do not know what 'X' is?" Now floating in the same boat with the letter writing, I knew the answer, but couldn't get it out of me in written form.

I didn't understand the process of writing the letters, even though I had sat in front of Samantha as she explained it to me. I did not know where to start. Just like in Algebra, I needed to do the same thing to both sides of the equation to solve the "X". I realized I needed help with Samantha's letter-writing process. I wanted to talk with someone who had been through it before. Here is the catch with that idea, Samantha is a therapist. I couldn't ask her for the names of people she worked with—that would be a serious privacy violation. I needed to leverage a common person—and I had an idea of who that person would be.

I needed to get a hold of a person named Heather. Heather, a 30-something, tall female, had a very big heart. At the time, Heather ran a couple of Meetup groups at the Holistic Lighthouse. Heather also studied psychology and had not completed her master's degree yet. I emailed Heather asking her for help. We set up a phone call. I really did not want to do this over the phone but acquiesced. I explained my problem. Apparently, I wasn't the letter-writing Lone Ranger. Everyone had this very problem. I had to admit I felt relieved to know it wasn't just me, but I still needed help. No one likes to sit in the corner with the dunce hat on.

Samantha had given me a handout to explain all the requirements for the letter. I looked at it—and it just did not click in my head. I made this much harder than it needed to be. I have a tendency of doing that very thing—thus, I can be my worst enemy. I hired Heather to help me. We rented office space for an hour at the Holistic Lighthouse. With Heather's help, I finally got it, but I decided I needed to do something first.

I now had a firm grip on how and what I would write in my first letter, but I wanted to do something else for a bit. I felt pretty haggard out about the letter-writing issue. Now I knew why Samantha made such a big deal about the letters and her process. I needed a short distraction to clear my mind of frustration I felt about starting my first letter.

Something that Samantha had said during her "Law of Attraction" event got me thinking. Samantha is big into "The Lord's Prayer". It didn't resonate with me. Samantha had a unique take on "The Lord's Prayer". Like Samantha, I had some ideas about how I could rewrite it to fit my current thoughts.

I know I should have been writing my letters, but I could not get this idea out of my head. I just needed to do this so I could move into the letter writing. I had told Samantha that for me to believe or buy into something I needed to make it my own. Since I needed to start the creative juices flowing, I thought this mini-project would give me a win before I got into the heavy lifting of my letter writing. I wanted to make "The Lord's Prayer" mine—and here is what I came up with:

Thank you Omnipotent life source.

Thank you for your divine guidance, protection, and blessings.

Please allow me the strength to let go of less optimum behavior patterns.

With this new path, watch as I walk the path, to the most optimum results for me.

Assist me in being able to lift myself to my optimum level that it is contagious to others, to open the idea of the most optimum path and blessings.

Please remind me through actions to be aware of forgiveness, understanding, judgments, and apathy.

Please allow the illumination of the path to transform me into my blessings.

I welcome the love, joy, and my shortfalls of your divine energy and to continue my path of "I think, therefore I do."

"The Lord's Prayer" is now mine to keep, and I go back to this version every once in a while. It reminded me where I was at with religion and my current thinking about it. I still to this day do not understand "why" I needed to do this; I just felt pulled in that direction. Being less resistant to change allowed expanded thoughts, which would otherwise have been drowned out, to come to the forefront of my mind and be acted upon.

So, time to get back to the letter-writing exercise and hopefully a successful outcome. I had the creative juices flowing. As I began writing, I had streams of tears running down my cheeks and onto my keyboard. I am glad I did not do this with a pencil and paper because the paper would have been soaked. This process became incredibly personal and painful. I do not know if they do something like this in Alcoholics Anonymous or not, but if you want a point to be driven home, this is a good way to do it. I knew the letter-writing process worked because in my mind I said to myself, *"This is written down. I do not have to hold onto this painful moment anymore."*

One would think that this process might be easy, but if you go deep and admit the hurt that happened in your life, there is nothing easy about it. It is like you look into the mirror and see these events unfold right before your eyes. The reflection on yourself doesn't lie or feel afraid. These events did happen. Now you acknowledge them and politely ask them to go away and never come back.

I finally figured out why I felt so stuck at the beginning of the letter-writing process. I thanked Heather for helping me along with a successful solution. I just had a mental block since I had been attempting to write the letter from a grown man's perspective and not the little boy with all of those behavior problems. Once I got past it, the letter wrote itself.

The process of writing the letters goes like this:
- **Introduction – Issue**
- **Paragraph #1 – Restore**
- **Paragraph #2 – Perception**
- **Paragraph #3 – Forgiveness**
- **Paragraph #4 -- End Result**

At the beginning of the letter, you state the person and actions that hurt you. You write from the perspective of the past—and this has nothing to do with the present or future.

The next paragraph is the restore paragraph. The restore paragraph allows you to take back what had been taken from you. You write very strong in this paragraph.

After the restore paragraph you have perception. This paragraph is where you add your input. This is what you did to extend or expand the negative feelings or actions. You have to be very honest here. You have to write from the time period of the problem. You don't hide the truth from yourself or make excuses.

The next paragraph is forgiveness. This paragraph allows you to forgive the person. There is a big difference in forgiving someone and letting them off the hook for their actions or words. For you to let go, you need to forgive them. You can walk away after that. You no longer need to hold onto the hurt, because there is no reason to hold on to it anymore.

After the forgiveness paragraph comes the end result or purpose of the resolution of the hurt paragraph. This is where you admit the end results of their actions toward you and your involvement in it.

In my first letter's last paragraph I had to admit that through my interactions I became a stronger, more resilient, more respectful, and more confident person. I succeeded beyond the hurt and now I am stronger for it. I have nothing to feel ashamed about or look to the past to try and change things.

If at that time I could know what I know now, my life would have been a lot easier. Life is not fair. The quicker I discovered this, the better my life would have been. It is too bad that it took me the majority of my life before this idea came to roost and settle into reality. I think we can all feel these feelings in ourselves if we are truly honest about it. Perception is a moment-by-moment thing. No one can dictate perception for another person.

In preparation for reading my letter to Samantha, I thought long and hard about what I was doing. I would reveal some very painful events in my life and my true feelings surrounding them. Yes, I wrote about the little Scott, but that did not stop the emotions from erupting all over the place.

As I read the letter to Samantha, I cried the whole time but I slugged through it. I had a pile of tissues on the floor when I finished. In the end, if I hadn't been honest and truthful about the events in my life, I believe it would not have worked for me. I needed to release those memories and forgive those who hurt me and move on with my life. Among the people who had hurt me was me. When you hate yourself, no one can love you. You just reject them and their heartfelt love for you.

I cleaned up all the tissues once I finished reading my letter. I even felt that picking up all the tissues from the floor and throwing them in the waste basket was therapeutic. This process is amazing. Samantha sat very neutrally during my reading. I felt surprised, but I think that if she showed emotion, it would have detracted from the reading. Samantha quietly told me that the letter had been a good letter. I would not need to do a rewrite. I felt truly grateful. A huge weight lifted off my shoulders. I really did not want to relive the writing of my first letter.

Writing my next letter was not as hard as the first one. The text flowed out of me pretty easily. The letter's content surprised me. I used a free-writing technique where I put down anything that came to mind on a piece of paper. Then I used it as my outline. I timed this free-writing process to keep me focused on the task at hand. This process differed from my first letter. I had learned a few things about writing these letters from my first endeavor. I wanted to try these techniques out on the second letter.

A couple of things stood out in the second process. I had sometimes been a pretty rotten kid. I had felt hurt so I had lashed out a lot. I simply did not understand as little Scott what people had been trying to do for me. Little Scott felt frustrated that he did not know how to read until the third grade. Little Scott fought a lot and took out his frustrations on others with ease. I am honestly surprised I did not end up in jail for beating people up who made fun of me. At the time I had been unable to hold back my anger when other kids laughed at me.

In the end, I only wrote two letters. I exhausted all my hurt feelings and released and forgave everyone. I had no other skeletons in my closet left to play with. After talking with Samantha about it, I did not see the need to try and make smaller issues into mountains. I put in the effort, and got rewarded with less suffering and more letting go.

I worked with Samantha for a couple more sessions before we both felt that I graduated from her process. In those last sessions, Samantha wanted to broach the subject of "chasing the divine" with me. "Chasing the divine" meant how after my cycling career had ended, how I had jumped into extreme sports and had done so with such a passion. The rock climbing, white-water kayaking, skydiving, motorcycle racing, and my 24-hour endurance car racing—all part of the chase. She came out and said that no one does these extreme activities unless they are chasing something. She thought she knew my motives. Her "chasing-the-divine" theory suggested I attempted to get back to where I had been while I raced bikes and experienced the endorphin high I had gotten from winning bike races.

I had become an endorphin junkie or addict. I willingly risked it all to get there again. This "feeling" became my crack. There is no 12-step program for this type of unhealthy risk-taking. I needed to spend some time looking at this issue. I really examined my true motivation for constantly risking my life—and in some cases, watching my friends die doing it. Yes, I had friends die doing activities that they loved. I understood the risks and so did they. I reasoned that in the end you are responsible for your actions one way or another.

This mental effort that looked into my true motivations moved me further down the road on my journey. I started to quit chasing the divine. Instead, I considered how I could help others get a small glimpse of the divine by reaching their goals. I started to call this effort in helping others a "halfway house for retired endorphin junkies".

The time I had spent with Samantha had been a very special and emotionally opening time for me. Working Samantha's process laid down the foundation of change for other shifts to help take me the rest of the way. The outer skin of the onion had been peeled away now and that caused a lot of watering eyes.

Time for more surgery and to leave behind the 12-pound sledge-hammer.

MINDFULNESS

A couple of weeks after Mark passed away I found peace with what had happened. Everyone has their time on Earth—and when it is up, it is up. It still hurts, but no one has the power to undo death. I can remember a short saying that moved and resonated with me. "Bad things happen to really good people." Sometimes the universe works against you or it has other plans for you. I saw myself in the "Other Plans" category.

Since I got through the Reiki training I wondered what else could be out there for me to discover. There had been a lot of buzz about a term called "mindfulness" and how it works. I felt really confused about all this talk, but no one could explain what is mindfulness. I searched the Internet for examples or explanations of mindfulness and all of them came up short for me. It was like an inside joke, and I was on the outside. I went back to my online classes and entertainment site and found a free mindfulness class created by a guy named Per. Hey with a name like Per, how could I ever go wrong? So, I dove in and attempted to understand mindfulness.

Unlike the Reiki class, I did not slam through it. I patiently did all the exercises and read the extra content. This course had a huge impact on me from a personality standpoint and in an inner calmness kind of way. Since I suffer from being a type-A personality, I had the unhealthy blood pressure to go with it. Throughout all of this process, I became more calm, present, and aware of my feelings. Since I lived in the present without actually realizing it, I started to see things differently. Small things didn't get to me anymore, and my coworkers and friends made comments about the changes in me. My wife also saw a new calmness in me. I changed in plain sight like a time-lapse video. I thought that if I fixed myself, then I could work with others to better understand them and create deeper relationships.

Mindfulness is something difficult to do but a simple concept, which accounts for the confusion around it. I wasn't the only one scratching my head around the concept of mindfulness. Mindfulness asks that you be present and understand that you cannot do anything about the past. The past has already happened. Now you can't do anything about it or the future since it hasn't happened yet.

Once I came to understand those concepts, I started to ask myself a few simple questions. Why are you worried about the future if it has not happened yet? Are you building a wall in front of you or is it already there? I am not saying reflecting about past or future events is all bad, it is just "what" past or future events you reflect on that matters. For me, I constantly replayed the winning of my first bike race. I had become stuck like the character in the television show *Married with Children*. The character Al Bundy constantly reflected on the greatest athletic achievement of his life, which happened to be when he scored five touchdowns in a single football game. I did not want to become Al Bundy nor did I want anyone else to think I acted like him. I guess deep down I did care what other people thought.

As I reached these conclusions and applied mindfulness to my life, it had a strange effect on me. I started to realize that I smiled more. I had gratitude toward other people and understood their actions better. I glowed outwardly and inside I had become very calm. I didn't have a care in the world. The mindfulness class taught by Per had a lasting effect that I have actually talked to him about.

I got in touch with Per because I wanted to thank him for putting up the free mindfulness class (gratitude is part of mindfulness). I figured the least I could do to was say I enjoyed the class and it had real value. Per's class lasted 12.5 hours with 91 lectures. A class that in-depth and detailed must have taken a while to put the content together.

Per suggested I read books his Zen Master referred to him, *Introduction to Zen Koans* and two Zen classics, *The Gateless Gate* and *The Blue Cliff*. These books offered a good start and eye-opening read. I started to realize I had become a Buddhist; I just did not call myself one. I soon decided Zen Buddhism was right for me.

After I had read the two classic books, Per offered what I consider to be his best book suggestion. This book spoke to me and answered so many questions about where I was on my journey. The book *The Mind Illuminated* by John Yates Culadasa provided a great explanation and plan of attack to deal with what I called "Monkey Brain" while meditating. The book explained the levels of attainment and the pitfalls to gaining a calmer inner peace.

The book surprised me. One would think that finding your inner calm would be a good thing. This is not always the case. Sometimes your meditation practice brings up negative feelings or emotional issues. You in some ways go backward before you can go forward. I thought it was just the opposite. You meditate and have all these positive feelings, but I soon discovered that wasn't always the case—especially for me.

Of all the books, I suggest people read this one. The other two books did not speak to me as strongly as *The Mind Illuminated*. I have a better understanding of things now. I also made every effort not to rush through the books, but to enjoy them as they unfolded.

LYNN

In December of 2017, I completed my work with Samantha. Now I needed to talk to someone with a different skillset. I had dealt with my early life issues. I also got a good dose of reality about my extreme sports activities. I had been able to put a wooden stake into the heart of most of those problems. I felt good about my work with Samantha—and I had worked with her as long as I possibly could.

Time to move on to the next phase. So, I started my Internet search for a new therapist. I began to think that I needed to develop a critical path in my mental development. I wanted to continue working along that path. This way, I could potentially minimize the amount of time with the therapist and reach my goals faster.

I quickly decided it would be a bad idea for me to try and take control of the process. The universe had been doing a good job of pointing me in the right direction and putting me in places where I could interact with others. This interaction brought Lynn to me in a chance meeting at the Lighthouse. After a few emails and phone conversations with Lynn on what I looked to do, I set up my first appointment with her in a rented office space at the Holistic Lighthouse. Lynn started working out of the lighthouse just after I completed my therapy with Samantha.

I chose Lynn as my next therapist for a couple of reasons. I evaluated her skillset and found that I could talk and relate to her. I also found her to be proactive in the therapeutic relationship. When I say proactive I do not mean pushy. She wants the best for the people she works with. I picked Lynn because she knew nothing about me. Her contact with Samantha at the Lighthouse had been very limited. I wanted to start with Lynn on a clean slate, which is exactly what I did. I created a new baseline with all of the old issues as solved issues. I also wanted to avoid someone jumping to conclusions because they had seen me at a Lighthouse event or they had previously talked to me.

Lynn was also a nurse, so I could talk about my health issues and the inner workings of all the prescriptions I took. Since I felt over-prescribed the medications became a hot topic. I wished to compete again, but didn't want to fool myself. Remember my philosophy, *I am responsible for my actions one way or another*. Deciding on my own to take myself off a medicine that in the end could do harm to my heart was not a good idea either in the short or long terms. Lynn's knowledge in the health area added great value to our therapeutic relationship. I had a lot of questions. I just needed someone to translate for me and explain why my treatment plan went one way and not the other.

Lynn also possessed different tools than Samantha. I wanted a different type of sounding board. I needed someone to help process my negative or emotional feelings as they were coming up a lot more because of my new meditation practice. Just like the "Law of Attraction," the more you think about something the more aware you are of it coming true. I had noticed I had been judgmental toward people and not fully listening to certain people. I also drove to and from work and would just break into crying spells.

These crying spells happened just out of the blue with no good reason. It seemed the happier that I got with myself, the more I had crying fits. I had let go of a lot of chatter and "Monkey Brain," which caused these spells. I had already acknowledged the inappropriate feelings in my conscious mind and asked them to go away. Now that the easy stuff had been vanquished, the deeper emotions or thoughts came to the surface.

I like to think of the conscious mind as a boardroom and the subconscious mind as the workers down below. The loudest worker gets the attention of thoughts from the boardroom and grabs the whiteboard to have at it. The book *The Illuminated Mind* covers this topic. I just needed to accept that these things would be happening as I develop as a meditator.

Lynn started with an introductory meeting in January 2018 when she got a feeling for what I wanted to do. I remember as I described the therapeutic situation I wanted, Lynn inquisitively looked at me. She didn't understand. I knew what I needed to do but had a problem communicating it to her. I wanted to talk things out and be questioned on my motivations and my feelings and actions. I intended to build on the work I did with Samantha, just in finer detail. Lynn would be the finishing hammer to Samantha's 12-pound sledgehammer. I also wanted to use the right tool for the right job, and I thought Lynn could help with that.

Lynn uses techniques that through action, you can reverse or reject negative feelings. The first technique we tried was the Emotional Freedom Technique (EFT). With EFT you tap certain points on your body in order to reinforce positive feelings. As we worked with EFT, I would make a declarative statement and repeat it as I tapped on the points.

The points are:
- The top of the head
- The eyebrow at the beginning of the eyebrow
- The side of the eye
- Under the eye
- Under the nose
- On the chin
- The collarbone
- Finally, under the underarm.

I found the concept of EFT kind of interesting. I willingly tried anything. This technique was something a little different than I had tried before. I think EFT works if the person doing it believes in it. There needs to be some personal buy-in with it—and therapists need to have confidence in what they do.

I wanted to explore EFT a little bit and try something different. I remember attempting to use different points that were acupressure points. I wanted to use more meaningful points that correspond with the body's energy flow. If you have emotional issues, doesn't it make sense to use emotional acupressure points? I also wanted to slow things down and set my intention to work and focus on the problem or issue. I thought too much and tried to get creative.

Using creativity for a technique, I personally believe is a good thing, as long as it's on your time. When you work with a therapist who attempts to steer you through an activity like this one, being creative is not helpful at all. It creates a power struggle and a divide between therapist and client. In this case, Lynn put a stop to my creativity—it didn't help. It hurt the flow of the technique—and I thanked her for doing so. It is not easy to redirect me because of my strong will. In the end, I made a mistake. If I wanted to get creative, I needed to do it at home. We needed to complete this process, and then I could do it differently on my own.

So my creativity being a nonstarter with Lynn got her to encourage me to stay the course with the program's original design. In the end, my issues continued to resolve using EFT, so I can't complain. In my opinion, many things can be added to the EFT technique to help people further explore their issues. I also found it funny that later on when I looked into the points for EFT, that they were actual acupuncture points for emotional release or control. I was indeed onto something; however, I had leapt before I actually knew how it worked.

Another technique Lynn uses involves a device that you sit on that vibrates to a frequency. I was also new to this technique.

You turn the device on and adjust the frequency of the vibrations to be the most in tune with you that day. I thought too much about doing this. Again, I have a habit of making things more complicated than they need to be. Lynn instructed me to just find a frequency that felt right and close enough counts. I think she threw in the "close enough counts" to hurry me along and not have me think too much. Lynn always acted pleasant, but we only had an hour to work with during our sessions together so she pushed. The device looked like a short extension cord with ends on both sides and a control unit wired into the middle of it. We used the device a couple of times, but I had to tell her that it made me want to go to the bathroom and I preferred to talk.

Lynn was a little disappointed and I think let down, but I did not see the value in using the device. Lynn explained that the device has a calming effect and helps people open up. I was not having problems opening up. After working with Samantha, I had no need to make more effort to open up. I directly answered all questions and openly expressed what I felt. This is another time where I needed to advocate for myself—and even though I decided to try all things and be open to it, if it is not working, move on.

I am sure the device works for most people, it just is not right for me. Some people in therapy have trouble opening up, so for them the device has value. Working with Lynn during our sessions was a little different but quite successful. I found it interesting that this therapy enabled me to solve my issues by the next session. Most of my issues revolved around negative thoughts, interactions with challenging people, and my meditation practice. I solved or self-corrected my issues between our sessions—and I felt happy about that. I honestly did not want anything as painful as the letter writing in this go-round of therapy.

Working with Lynn resulted in every session being like the first one. We rapidly burned through my "need-to-work-on" items, which meant no need to go any further with more sessions. Our rapid success probably shocked Lynn since it didn't require as much effort to accomplish our goals. However, the ease in which my items melted away limited our time together. While I fully believe that I needed to work with someone like Lynn, it just felt a little funny doing it. This "every-day-is-a-new-day" therapy seemed a bit different but also slightly frustrating. However, it succeeded and that is what matters.

After I finished with Lynn, I did not seek out a new therapist for quite a while. In my next round, I wanted to find a special person (as always). I didn't feel sure a new therapist offered the right way to go. I craved feedback, not for validation but to challenge my new belief system. I needed an athletic person who knew how to fight for what he/she believed in. Since I didn't connect with anyone, I would have to walk the road alone on this portion of my journey. I also needed to let all the things I worked on with Lynn settle in. We moved through so many things that I needed some time to process it all.

MEETUPS

Since I spent so much time at the Holistic Lighthouse their social events drew me in. I did not know it at the time, but some of the events I went to were actually Meetup groups. Meetup is an Internet-based organizing and meeting place. People create a Meetup to talk about mutual interests such as knitting, tarot cards, or my favorite, meditation.

You find Meetups by using their app or website. Once you create an account you can start searching for topics of interest. Since I tried to meet new people and get out of my comfort zone by experiencing new things, Meetups offered an ideal place to explore. Meetup groups offer a lot of diversity of ideas and things to do, not to mention meeting some really interesting people.

Yes, some of the Meetups are a little "wack-a-doodle" or woo-woo, but that is exactly the point. I needed to meet special people who walk to different drummers. In a way, I wanted to use Meetups to discover what I thought was important or unimportant. I know this sounds off from what I'm discussing in the book, because this journey should be an introspective process and not grounded in groupthink. I am not a big fan of groupthink—and for the most part, I think groupthink offers a weak way of reasoning, but it seemed right for this situation.

I visited the Meetup site and found out they had a phone app. I downloaded the app on my cell phone and started looking around at the different groups. I wanted to start with a geography search because it made no sense to travel a great distance for a common Meetup subject. An example of a common subject would be a workout Meetup or a meditation Meetup. I started searching for groups that interested me. I also promised myself that even if the Meetup that I signed up for was wacky, I would see value in it—at least from the group leader's perspective. I considered this respectful. I honestly did not want to prejudge anything. I would be a guest in their house and act accordingly.

My first Meetup came a few nights later. The Meetup, much to my surprise, was called "The Meaning of Life". Wow! I hit pay dirt. I could start this part of the journey from the comfortable place—one I was educated about. Life philosophy wasn't new to me, which broke my rule a bit; however, the people were new. The subject honestly interested me. I only considered this a baby step since I only tiptoed out of my comfort zone. What more could a college philosophy student ever want? Turns out, I assumed wrong.

I showed up at the Holistic Lighthouse for the event. They channeled me into a small room with six ladies already present. When I entered the room the ladies quickly stopped talking and noticed me. I did not find this rude or feel like they looked at me with suspicion. I got the general impression they welcomed me to the group even though I happened to be a guy and they had never seen me before at the Lighthouse.

The room, the same size as the therapy room, didn't offer a lot of space. Now, I promised myself that I would be open to anything, so I took my seat in the corner. While sitting there, I decided that I would not be a wallflower so I made some small talk with the group. I took special care to talk with everyone in the room and try to pay equal attention to each person. I did not want to alienate anyone on my first day in the group. I know how I can be when it comes to meeting new people. I have a tendency to amp things up. I really did not want to stick out any more than I already did.

The Meetup started, and I had prepared myself to swim in the deep end of the pool on a lot of subjects. However, I quickly got taken off guard once I discovered the topics weren't what I anticipated. I had just jumped right out of my comfort zone. The ladies started talking about numerology and not Plato or Aristotle. I am pretty sure the ladies saw the shocked look on my face and then the blank stare. I had a hard time following along—and felt like I just got "pantsed" in the schoolyard. I finally said to myself, "Well I am here, I need to just go with the flow and I might just learn something."

The flow of the conversation quickly turned to aura reading, energy work, tarot cards, crystals, and people's special gifts. It only took about 10 minutes before the ladies asked my full name, birth date, and what city I was born in. They also quizzed me on my knowledge of the subjects at hand. I admitted I knew about Tarot, but did not have a set of cards. I also confessed I didn't own any crystals.

I answered the rest of their questions as quickly as I could in a staccato fashion. I felt a little concerned—I did not want to have the emphasis on me. The ladies though kept going full speed ahead. I felt like the "new book" in the book of the month club. Everyone wanted to read my numbers. I explained that while I felt nicely welcomed, I was only there as an observer. I wanted to learn about different subjects. The ladies would have none of that notion and started to run my numerology numbers.

While they worked out my numbers, they took turns explaining that the numbers associated with different traits and qualities in people. I found this interesting and just listened. Once my numbers were complete they all got very excited. I really did not understand why they were excited, because I am who I am and that is that. They took great glee in telling me that I was a "5" and even better a "5" with some "11s". It is not supposed to matter what your numbers are because they represent who you are, but some have a little more jazz behind them than others. I said, "Ok I am a 5 with some 11s, can anyone tell me why that is important?"

The ladies continued to talk amongst themselves and after a bit, I had to interrupt them asking what the fuss was about. I once again felt like I was on the outside looking in. They held out on me. They acted excited to have something and someone new to play with.

One of the ladies looked at me and said that each one of them had individual gifts. By reading my numbers they could tell what type of person I am. So, in the end, I discovered my number, 32/5.

I replied, "Ok, what do the numbers say about me, and what are my primary traits?"

They started to explain the meaning of the numbers, but I have included below a description of what my numbers mean from a website on the Internet.

SeventhLifePath.com is the website I found that gave me a good description of what my numbers mean. At the time of writing this the service was free. The website produces a very detailed report on your numbers and then emails it to you in a day or so. I thank the people at the SeventhLifePath.com site for my report.

Your Life Path is 32/5

The key to your personality is freedom. Scott, you love to travel, adventure, variety and meeting new people. You possess the curiosity of a cat and long to experience all of life. You love to be involved in several things at the same time as long as you are not tied down to any one area. You like change, new things, and new horizons. You make friends easily; your personality is upbeat and often inspiring attracting people from all walks of life. You have a way of words and an uncanny ability to motivate others. You can be in sales, advertising, publicity, promotion, politics or any profession that requires your communication skills and understanding of people. You likely lack discipline and order. You can also be impulsive, doing or expressing things you regret later. Scott, you are sensual and love to taste all of life. Sex, food and other sensory experiences are essential to the enjoyment of your life. You find it difficult to commit to one relationship, but once committed you can be as faithful as an old dog. You are multi-talented and possess a variety of diverse abilities. However, discipline and focus are the true keys to your success. Without these many of the tasks, you begin will remain unfinished and you will fail to realize the true fruits of your abilities. With hard work and perseverance, the sky is the limit. You may have been perceived as a wild child by adults and a source of concern by your family. However, do not be obliged to hurry for your choice of career. You are often a late-bloomer and need to experience life before you can truly know and commit to your heart's desire. Your challenge is to learn the true meaning of freedom. Change is constant in your world requiring adaptability and courage. Try to maintain an exercise program, keep your body in shape and limber. The flexibility and durability of your body will promote security and confidence within you. You yearn for freedom and self-employment attracts you powerfully. Your challenge is to settle into one area to cultivate your ability sufficiently to earn a living and attain success. Once you find your niche the motivation and inspiration you supply others will bring you much in return, you will find your friends and colleagues supporting and promoting you on the road to success.

Source SeventhLifePath.com

I thought the report came really close to my own reality or opinion of myself. There is something to numerology. I think it can be used to come up with a general idea about a person and how they act.

I had to admit to myself that I had a lot of information running through my head. It all sounded reasonable given the context of the Meetup. The conversation then turned on its head because one of the ladies, Angela just stared hard at me. The stare was not a mean-looking stare, it was an inquisitive stare. At the time I thought Angela wanted to say something but felt confused about how to approach me. After staring for a while, she let me know that one of her gifts enabled her to see people with letters and colors over them. Angela explained that I had two colors and two words associated with me and asked me if I wanted to know them. Just like me, she does not offer information unrequested out of respect for the individual. Some people just do not want to know. This way, you don't take people off guard or behave rudely.

I started to enjoy my new friends and their many gifts. I thought it would be fun to find out what she saw. I did not see the harm in any one of them expressing their opinions or findings about me. That is what I was there to do—and if I wanted to expand my awareness, I had to roll with the punches.

Angela said that I had the words "Self-Centered" in black and red above my head. The room went quiet and none of the ladies expected this to come out of Angela's mouth. I took a moment.

I was in uncharted waters with all of this new information. I looked at her and to her surprise, I replied, "I agree."

All the ladies stayed silent at my response. Then I attempted to explain to them what I thought. So much for flying under the radar and beating back the old Scott. I brought drama to the room, which was not my intention when I first walked into this Meetup. Since I was already there, I went ahead and moved forward with this conversation.

I started to speak about being a retired athlete and how all athletes revolve around their training schedules. I have been called self-centered before, and it did not shock me coming up now. I considered it part of the Meetup to explore all things categorized as the "Meaning of Life". This is one of the things I had been working on during my two-year journey. I spent a lot of time with Samantha and Lynn discussing how I could move on from my past athletic accomplishments and not have them be the main focus of my life. Also, this is not the first time someone had questioned me about this subject. I always try not to take anything personally.

As an athlete you spend a lot of quality time training. I explained that my daily training ride had between five- or six-hours long. By default, if you want to be successful, success is done in training and executed at the different racing events. I used to race 100 to 120 times a year. Training has to come first—and no other priorities matter.

Now, five or six hours takes up a good chunk of time so something in your life needs to budge to accomplish your goals. Time is fixed. You only have 24 hours in a day, and you need to prioritize training to fit the important things into the day. This means not doing things with friends and time away from the girlfriend. This is why athletes think of themselves first, and what it will do to their training schedule before making a decision. I explained, "No one gave me a spot on the U.S. National Cycling Team. I earned it with hard work and dedication." I said it with some intensity to get my point across. So much for keeping a low profile and not throwing ego into it.

Interestingly enough, no one blinked an eye at my candor. They all understood where I came from. I continued to talk about my reaction at being called "self-centered" by Angela. I expressed that in attempting to be open and honest with people I do not get upset when someone calls me a name or thinks I am full of it. I said, I had been working on myself to make myself better. I stressed that I had also let the universe steer for a while, and it seemed to be working. "This is how I came to be with you tonight," I said. In a joking fashion, I added, "Congratulations! You have me for tonight's entertainment."

As it turned out red and black mean something, too. I did some digging, and it appears that the color red can be interpreted with passion and drama. I definitely brought drama to the group, but I will go with passion on this one because I do not like drama. The drama was the second thing I dropped from my life once I decided on taking my two-year journey. The first one was guilt. I do not do guilt, as nothing good ever comes from feeling guilty. I feel guilt is a wasted experience that no one likes. Other words associated with red are it attracts attention, strong emotion, danger, courage, strength, power, and a strong link to sexuality.

Black is associated with hiding emotions, implies a barrier, sophisticated, sexy, secretive, power and control, and confidence. I can agree with Angela seeing colors. I was still in that place of competition and not fully letting go, but I tried to let it all go. I had been self-centered, and I had acted that way all of my life.

I felt pretty good about the Meetup and the feedback I got from the ladies. I honestly learned something I never would have learned left to my own devices. I did pick up some tarot cards and a book on them, used crystals in some Reiki sessions, and paid attention to people's given names for numerology. I did not go too far with these items, as I felt that my new ability to read people, or put another way, get a vibe from them, told me all I needed to know about them. If I got a bad vibe, I would steer away. Life's too short for negative people. If I got a good vibe I would openly engage them and be present with them.

PAST LIVES JANE

There were many Meetup group leaders, but I really appreciated Heather's Meetups. Yes, she helped me jumpstart my letters for Samantha, but she usually had a good topic to talk about or an exercise to work on to better understand yourself. Heather's topics varied from week to week. After a while, I really did not care about the topic, because I knew it would be new. One of the last Meetups I did with Heather was a past-lives-regression meditation.

At this Meetup, I showed up on time as usual. Heather did not have anything officially slated for the day. The Meetup was supposed to be a meditation. She was not prepared or interested in doing that meditation because she felt physically and mentally tired. Heather works in healthcare. She had been working a lot, so I did not make any kind of fuss about it. She decided to freestyle the Meetup and asked the group if we wanted to do a recorded past-lives-regression meditation.

Heather let us know that she had recently purchased several meditations on varying topics from the app store, and she loved this past-lives meditation in particular. I honestly did not believe in past lives and actually thought it was bunk. I thought it was the subconscious associating things that had happened or wished had happened to the conscious mind. Since I promised myself that I would try pretty much anything and I was already there, that I would go with the flow—and I am glad I did. Since it was Heather's Meetup, it should be good and worth my time. She had not failed me yet.

They held the meditation in the main classroom in the back of the Holistic Lighthouse. The room, a rectangular shape, had dark-red and brown colors. The room gave visitors a warm and welcoming feeling. It had a few wall pictures and one large whiteboard to write on. Industrial-grade, square carpet covered the floor and offered little comfort to lie on, but it did stand up to high foot traffic. Since we all brought yoga mats, the floor worked fine.

The meditation started with all of us lying on our yoga mats. It gave an introduction to tonight's meditation. Since we laid in the spacious, main classroom the six participants had enough room to spread out and give each other space. My thin mat didn't protect me against the cold concrete floor, which gave me a slightly strange feeling, but nothing too unpleasant.

As the meditation began, it used a recorded male voice that instructed us about the five stages. I remember thinking that this would be different. Although I had already prejudged the meditation, I reminded myself to be open-mined about what might happen.

After the introduction to the meditation, the male voice guided us into relaxation and inspection of tension in our bodies. All meditations that I have done first start with quieting the body and mind and then working on the meditation's intention. When you meditate on something like past lives it makes it easier to set your intention before you start. I set my intention to be open and honest with myself and allow myself to go back into my brain and remember any past lives that wanted to come forth. To be honest, I had no other option for my intention because I have never re-lived a past life, and it never crossed my mind to do so.

I succeeded in relaxing my body, which has always been easy for me to do. I am very aware of my body and what it does. I really hear my heartbeat. I could hear it slow to the low 50 beats per minute. I use my heartbeat as a constant reminder that I am alive and need to be present in my thinking and dealing with other people. After the body-relaxing stage, we moved into the actual meditation. The meditation was set up with five active stages of five minutes each. Between stages the meditation took a break to enable you to self-reflect or recover from what you just experienced during the different stages.

In stage one, the narrator asked several questions but the first question asked: "Where are you?" and my brain immediately responded "New York City." I was shocked—this answer came out of nowhere. I have only been to New York City once when I had a bike race in Central Park in 1984. I had a very strange feeling before the question came. It felt like hesitation and then a feeling came over me. It felt like I sunk into the concrete floor about four inches each time the narrator asked a question. I found this sensation very strange. I started to get concerned since I broke into a sweat—and that sweat later became a cold sweat from the floor's coolness. Then I once again sank into the concrete four inches and the narrator asked me my name and my mind immediately responded "Janet." I said to myself this is getting a little freaky. This safe space allowed me to explore things, but this experience got me out of my comfort zone. I sank into the concrete floor again as the narrator asked what year it was and my brain immediately responded 1934.

"Ok, this is just strange," but I remembered as a kid that I used to believe I would die at age 34. I know this is not a normal thought, but I truly did think that something was going to happen when I turned 34 and it would end my life. I vividly remember those dreams. I know this sounds odd but over time I grew to accept it. I made so many risky decisions doing extreme sports in my life based on the idea that I would not survive after age 34.

The meditation continued and I visualized a skyscraper-like building. I focused on the right side of the building and the third window from the right. My focus shifted to me being outside of the building, and I was falling. I looked at the building. I noticed a glassed-in observatory platform. I saw a girl in a blue dress. She looked to be between the ages of 10 to 12. I immediately understood that she was my daughter. She witnessed my death from either jumping or being thrown off the building. The details in this recollection amazed me. I can still recall it today.

I have reflected on this vision. I do not have any feelings either way about whether someone threw me or I jumped off the building. The meditation phase one ended with me seeing "Janet" (as I realized that was her name) from above. Janet died on top of a car parked below. The narrator began to speak, and I felt a sensation of coming out of the floor, and I lost my cold sweat and goosebumps.

Before the narrator came back on after the break I sank back into the floor again, and experienced the same goosebumps and cold sweat. The narrator announced that we had jumped five years ahead in time and asked, "Where are you?" This time I did not get an answer in my head. I immediately saw a white light and the light shone for a very long time. I wasn't able to make out any details of my surroundings, so I kept my eyes closed, but the goosebumps and the cold sweat hung around for the ride. When the white light finally began to clear I could focus again, and I was in a room.

I was underground somewhere. I saw a lot of plaster arches and figures. The figures were of people, but they were just the outlines of the people with no movement. The arches were like an old-world church you might find in Europe. They had some decorations on them. The color scheme, an assortment or white blends, reds, oranges, and tans, reminded me of pictures of Tuscany, Italy.

I soon realized I was dead. This place was where my body had been placed. I have never seen a room like this one that I can remember, so I didn't know how I imagined something I have never been exposed to. I began to feel myself rising out of the floor, and my goosebumps and cold sweat subsided.

The narrator spoke again and announced that it was five years later and asked the question, where are you? I did not have a response. I experienced calm silence; I just had a visual of a mausoleum with the same colors as before.

I had a hard time keeping the visualization going in this stage. I kept coming back out of the meditation and then going back in. I did not gain anything meaningful from this stage of the meditation except I came out of it crying. I cried for no good reason. I felt a little befuddled because there was no rational reason for me to be crying. This just added to the mystery of this meditation. I remember asking myself, "Am I really doing this?"

When the narrator came back on, I just let the tears run down my cheeks and attempted to deal with the tension that newly afflicted me. My body became full of stress. I felt it not just in one area like my back or neck; it was an all-over body feeling. It took me a while before I could get most of the muscles to relax enough to participate in the meditation. It felt like being in a fight or flight mode, but the room presented no danger that I could see.

The narrator once again announced that we have moved five more years in the future. I went back in and felt myself sinking into the floor and the goosebumps and a cold sweat came back. I immediately felt like someone stood over me. I opened my eyes, but there was no one there. I thought maybe Heather had been walking around the room checking in with people, but when I looked over, she laid on the floor and had not moved.

After closing my eyes again, I started to visualize a room as you would find in the early rings of *Dante's Divine Comedy*. This is also known as *Dante's Inferno*. I saw in my visualizations a lot of tan stone and very old architecture. I also saw black and white shapes moving around the room. The shapes looked like old pictures of Puritans—I thought that seemed strange. I am as far from being a Puritan as you can get, so the visualization got lost a bit in translation. I decided that the meditation had fallen apart. I was already dead and had been dead for a very long time. Before the narrator could speak again, I already came back on top of the concrete and the goosebumps and cold sweat subsided. I had lost the meditation, and my focus had gone all over the place.

For the fifth and final stage, I did not go back in. I had a very uneasy feeling that someone had been standing over me. I felt haunted by it. I kept my eyes open the whole time. I did not want to close my eyes either. I wanted the lights to come on as I had a growing sense of anxiety. My whole body felt like it went into lockdown. The tension came back and I couldn't shake it off. I tried really hard to not squirm or make any noise, but I looked around the room for who or what stood or hovered over me. I did not see anyone. I just sensed something. I thought my mind played tricks on me.

During the last phase of the meditation, I started to reflect on it and became aware of several things. First, I am afraid of heights, which is why I started rock climbing and skydiving. I had been also haunted by the year 1934. I had to ask myself the obvious question: "Could my dreams about dying at age 34 really be because of a past life?" To me, this question had a simple answer and that is, yes.

After the meditation ended I become silent and quietly withdrawn. Most of the group started opening up about their experiences. They unfortunately experienced nothing during their past-lives meditation. Heather finally asked me what I experienced. I reluctantly talked, but I started to explain my meditation by saying, "You are never going to believe this, but ..." I described what had happened in the meditation by stages and quickly got my journal out and wrote down as much about the meditation that I could remember. I really wanted to document this meditation because it had been strange but wonderful.

Here is what I wrote:

I am happy I did the meditation because it exposed me to what was possible if you just open up your mind and let it flow. I have purposely taken the position that I have had past lives even though I originally did not believe in them. I can admit when I am wrong but there were simply too many factors and vivid details to what I experienced during the meditation. It is sort of a shame that I was not open to this type of experience before, I just had no first-hand experience with past lives to base my opinion on. I was walking around and not seeing what was in front of me. In reflecting on the tension and the feeling I had someone standing over me, maybe there was something there? I cannot tell you what it was, but there was something there. I know some have the ability to see spirit guides and such. I do not have that gift and the most obvious would have been the spirit of Janet which gives me goose bumps just thinking about it.

FLOAT THERAPY

After doing several Meetups I wanted to do something different than meditation and new age adventures into the spirit world. The Meetups were sometimes a little "out there". The meetings exposed me to some great mind-expanding ideas, but I wanted something that would push me in a different direction. I wanted to further my intention, go deeper into my meditations, and let my mind expand in ways that I wouldn't normally go.

After exploring relaxation techniques, I found something called Float Therapy. Float Therapy combines a large sensory deprivation chamber or room and epsom-salt-infused water. Float therapy provides a way to cut yourself off from normal sensory experiences you have around you. When you cut out all the normal noise stimuli, you become more aware of what exists under all that racket. Since it takes you to a different level of awareness (if you allow yourself to go there) it can also become another mind-expanding experience.

A normal float therapy session starts with walking into your float-therapy room. The room consists of a changing area, a shower, and a door into the float-therapy chamber. After you shower, you enter a doorway into the float chamber and close the door behind you.

I want to stress that you are in control of the room and no one forces you to do anything, like keep the door closed. If you get claustrophobic, you can open up the door of the tank to regain your composure. The float therapy experience is supposed to be a relaxing one, not something that gives you anxiety or terror. You also do not need to use all the time given. A normal session is 60 minutes. You can get out of the tank at anytime during the typical session. Simply shower right there and get dressed to leave.

There are several types of float chambers. The clamshell design, which is what you commonly see in strip malls, enables you step into it and close the lid. Then you have the standing models, which allow you to stretch and wiggle around in the water. These kind are also not as claustrophobic as the clamshell-design rooms. I have gone to several float therapy locations, but my favorite location and tank, which has a lot of room in it, allows you to lie in the middle of the tank and not touch the sides. I can put my arms straight over my head and by my sides. The buoyancy of the epson-salt-infused water enables me to put myself in positions that would be difficult to do on the floor.

Once you are in the chamber and lying in the epson saltwater you literally semi-float. I say "semi-float" since most of your body sinks below the waterline, but you do not submerge completely into the water—and it doesn't cover your face. The water temperature is very close to body temperature, so your body feels very comfortable. You aren't too hot or cold. At some locations the temperature can be adjusted to suit your own comfort.

Float therapy works best if you open your mind to it. If you keep up your "filters", you will not fully experience the joy of floating. Settling into your float session you can experience anything under the sun. I see colors. I paint geometry on the walls. I have also self-illuminated and expanded beyond the float-therapy chamber. I know this sounds way out there, but when you feel truly relaxed and open your mind, strange and wonderful things can happen. You just have to allow it to happen. The human mind is an amazing thing. I have heard from other floaters that they see spirits or their guardian angels. Others have told me that they see colors and work out their emotional issues in silence. There is no wrong answer here; it is just what comes up. I have floated better than 100 times, and no two floats are alike.

Inside the tank, you are in complete darkness, but once your eyes adjust to the float-therapy environment you will actually see the slight differences in the surrounding area. You can call it different shades of black. Moisture in the air gives you the ability to blow into the air and see it move. One of my favorite things to do when I am in the float tank is to blow straight up into the air and watch the air current come back down the front wall and over my head. It looks like a Dementor attack from the Harry Potter series. I remember the first time I accidentally made this happen it took my breath away. Now I do it just for fun.

Now float therapy became a part of my new journey. I can just let my brain go when I do it. I equate it to meditation because of the absence of sensory input, which allows all of those conscious filters to drop. It gives the subconscious easier access to the conscious mind, which is where the fun begins. You just need to accept the idea that strange and wonderful things can and will happen. Some people have said that floating is like taking a halogenic drug. I will have to take these people's word for it since I have never dropped acid and shied away from illegal drugs.

Float Therapy was also referenced in the book *Stealing Fire* by Steven Kotler and Jamie Wheal. In the book, they looked at a Navy Seal team in which floating was a part of their training to increase their "flow". In the book, it also detailed the use of flow with Silicon Valley entrepreneurs and trendsetters. This letting go of conscious filters allowed entrepreneurs to make big and complex decisions with focus and clarity. Floating also allows you to make big decisions without regret.

I use float therapy to deal with undesirable emotions and honestly to check out from the daily grind. If I have had a rough day, getting a "floatie" offers a great way to deal with it. It allows me some perspective on issues—and by the end of the float, my issues are resolved.

As part of my journey, I knew that my emotional state had changed. The more I had control over my emotions in an organic kind of way, the more deeply I could meditate and enjoy the things that I felt passionate about. I used floating to clear my mind in the chamber and allow anything to come forward. This would be the same kind of thoughts that a beginning meditator might experience. Most people call it "Monkey Brain". I let the monkey out of its cage and allowed thoughts to dart in and out of my head. After a while, I would take an undesirable thought, acknowledge it, and tell it it's not an appropriate time to be thinking that thought. The sensory deprivation helped me since I didn't have any other stimulus to deal with. The absence of normal background noise made it easier to fight it. This accelerated my ability to deal with negative emotions and allowed me to reinforce positive ones. I had made a huge breakthrough. I got paid off with no more unexpected crying in my car on my way back home from work.

I also made a request when I am settled into the float chamber to be open to communications with anyone. Some people see spirit guides, but I do not have that gift. I do know that when I make the request, I soon have full-body goosebumps. Maybe one day with the goosebumps I can have a visual experience with my spirit guide or animal.

MASSAGE SCHOOL

I made a lot of progress with float therapy. My brain had become more open, and I felt less stress and anxiety. I found it easier to deal with my day job as a Systems Engineer and all the changes happening around me. I also started to want to share my positive experience with others about overcoming resistance to change—and I wasn't finished yet. I wanted to explore more.

Floating is a solo activity. I wondered what else I could do to bring a little relaxation to people and have it also have a mellowing side effect on me? One day the answer came to me. I was lying on a massage table in August 2017. I talked to my masseuse Vika about maybe looking into doing massage for athletes. My desire to share my newly acquired wisdom and help people pulled me toward the idea of helping athletes; plus, I had the skills to do so. If floating helped me with the after-effects of being an athlete, this could help transition people from their athletic careers to a normal life—especially since this transition is not always graceful for athletes.

I have had massages all my life. While I raced bikes I used to get a massage on a daily basis. Other non-race days I would do self-massage to get the lactic acid out of my legs before and after my daily training ride. It wasn't uncommon to find me lying on the floor with my legs propped up on a wall, letting gravity help me move blood out of my legs. This self-care act is really important to keep your legs fresh and feeling good.

When Vika had me flipped over to work on the front of me I asked her if I went to massage school did she think I would be any good at it? She smiled and said, "You have such good energy about you that I cannot see how you would not be any good at it." To my surprise, Vika then asked me if I wanted a massage table? I thought to myself *"what a wonderful gift."* Her generous offer also took me aback. I said, I would look into massage schools—and if I did sign up, I would let her know. Now massage people do not make a lot of money, and Vika was being very generous. A massage table of any quality costs around $200 and up. I wasn't about to take such a gift as a massage table and not use it for its intended purpose. Vika finished up my massage with a smile on her face the whole time. I think she knew that I would move forward and go to massage school.

It took me a few weeks, but I did settle on a massage school in Davis, Ca. Julie, the director of the school, had been running it since its inception. I got a good vibe from her and the school. I interviewed several other schools and wasn't happy with what I found. Many of the schools do not allow you to have another job, which wouldn't work for me. I wasn't going to quit my Systems Engineering job to attend massage school full time. I couldn't afford it, and if I tried my wife would have my head.

I needed some flexibility and none of the schools in Sacramento, Ca. area were flexible. They all wanted me to be available

Monday through Friday during business hours to attend classes. They also dictated which classes I had to take. I did not want someone picking my classes for me. I knew I would find a modality that interested me and focus on it. They also wanted double to triple the amount of money for a 500-hour Certified Massage Therapist program than the school in Davis wanted. This situation simply would not work for me. I am on a budget and my work schedule was locked in. Getting a student loan for something that is an experiment is just a silly notion. I needed to do this with on-hand cash. I signed up with the massage school in Davis and jumped in taking classes that interested me.

Since I was new to the school and I wanted to get started as quickly as possible, I came to the school a little sideways. I tend to do this—and it's not always a good thing. It is kind of like paddling upstream because you force a non-standard process in a standard world. I always make things more difficult than they need to be, and I did it again. Because of this non-standard approach, I had to take classes that did not have any class prerequisites.

Every massage student needs to take the "Massage Fundamentals" class as a prerequisite to the other classes. You cannot work on people with their clothes off until you take this class. So the average student takes it first and then progresses through the other classes. In California, you are required to take a 500-hour program if you want to work as a massage therapist. To work in my area you need your Certified Massage Therapist (CMT) certificate. With this goal in mind, I started working toward my

500 hours to finish my schooling. My excitement to get quickly started combined with the school's requirement to get through the classes in 500 hours in one year caused problems. It wasn't the school's fault either. I had missed this information in my rush to start. Now I had to search the course catalog for weekend classes that did not require any prerequisites.

My first class was an Ortho-Bionomy upper extremities class. I could not have started with a more difficult class, as most people consider Ortho-Bionomy an advanced modality. As I look back at this class I just cannot explain my decision-making except (once more) you cannot fix stupid—it's sad but true. The fundamentals of Ortho-Bionomy are simple, but the learning curve is very steep. In Ortho-Bionomy, you have a point of contention in the body and to deal with that contention you position or maneuver the person to build a cave around the contention point. Once you have done that you compress toward the point of contention to reset the muscle groups in the area. This is a 30,000-foot description of Ortho. If I get more specific, I would need a full book to do it justice.

On my first day of class, I walked into the small, three-room school and started to make small talk with everyone. I could not have been with a more accepting and supportive group of people. I felt a bit like an oddball—a true outsider in this environment. I probably imposed these feelings on myself, but it was my reality at the time. They accepted my rigidness, my nervousness. They were amazed that I chose this class of all the classes to be my first one.

Jim, the Ortho-Bionomy instructor, was a high-energy, nonassuming, super skinny guy who loved Ortho-Bionomy. As a Master Instructor, he can be found in many YouTube videos where he demonstrates Ortho-Bionomy. Jim, one of those quirky guys whose attitude is just infectious, truly wants you to be as successful as you can be. He has absolutely no ego. He walks the walk that he talks. He is not one of those stuffy instructors who is all about "do what I say, not as I do." This approach was very refreshing. I had too many egotistical instructors during my bachelor's and master's programs. Jim helped me feel welcome in my new, challenging environment. I call it challenging because I was brand, spanking new to all of this massage business. I did not know anything about Ortho-Bionomy when I walked in the door of the school. They listed the class in the course catalog and showed it required no prerequisites, so I jumped at the chance to get into it.

As with all classes, the instructor introduces himself first and gives a short bio. I did say short, didn't I? Well, Jim always had a lot to say—and it is pretty entertaining. Jim teaches at many schools. When you take a class from him, you do hear about his exploits along with the history of Ortho. Jim learned his skills from the creator of Ortho-Bionomy. In the end, I took six ortho classes from Jim, and I enjoyed five of them a lot. The one I did not enjoy was the class that I sat presently in.

After the introduction period I immediately felt lost—and it didn't get any better throughout the day. When it came time for my personal introduction, I kept it short. I said little more than my name is Scott and this is my first class. I did not want to embarrass myself anymore than I felt I would do. I don't normally feel self-conscious, but in this situation I stepped well out of my comfort zone.

Once the introductions were done, the real part of the class started. When it came time to partner up the terror set in. I got paired up with a working massage professional. Now survival became the plan for the day. I had fears of being eaten alive. I felt relieved when my partner, a woman, ended up helping me a lot. I panicked over all the new material and not having any feel for Ortho.

Jim though, a supportive instructor, encouraged me to stop thinking and trying so hard. He watched me, and he could see the gears in my head moving, which was not the desired effect. I focused too much on the task at hand and didn't absorb what was important, which was the *technique*. Jim kept stressing that I needed to feel out the issue and use my intuition. I needed to let myself go. It got lost in translation, as my "righties" and "lefties" got all tangled.

At the end of the class, it was standard practice for the class participants to circle up in the main classroom area and receive our class certificates. When I got my certificate, I proclaimed to the group, "I survived and I will be coming back for more." I guess I do like the abuse, pain, and suffering. I felt really excited that I survived. I looked forward to doing more classes with Jim. You know for someone who has jumped out of a plane skydiving over one-hundred times with two-night dives, I found that massage class to be pretty tough business. I left the school that day with a big headache, but a newfound appreciation for Ortho-Bionomy.

Weeks later, I used an Ortho-Bionomy maneuver on one of my coworkers. The coworker, a new database administrator for us at the hospital, had his neck locked up. Experiencing serious pain, he came over to my cubicle and asked if I could help him. I have to admit that I felt a little nervous to put hands on someone and help them with a modality that I barely understood, but I went for it anyway. What could happen? Worst-case scenario would be that if it did not work I would just say that I gave it a shot and I needed more Ortho classes.

I had my coworker stand in front of me with his back to me. I asked him to put his neck and head in the most comfortable position he could find. This move cheated, but I wanted my coworker to help me to help him. You would normally work on someone on a massage table or in a chair, but this was a neck issue. I did not think it mattered. My coworker complied, and I asked him for permission to go hands-on. (You never just put your hands on someone without asking for permission first.) Jim always talked about how you approach the client, especially if he/she is in pain. You do not want the person you try to help to guard against what you try to help him/her improve.

My coworker agreed to let me go hands-on. I soon found the spot, which was the center of pain. I micro-adjusted his neck and head to get the spot to soften up. Once I found the soft spot I applied a small compression on the top back part of his head. Then I compressed to the point of contention.

I smoothly made this non-violent action with little pressure. I dealt with someone's neck here, so I did not want to use too much pressure. I instructed my coworker to let the adjustment sink in a bit and not start to move his neck to see if the pain went away. I asked him to slowly turn his head to the right and then again to the right. Next I asked him to turn his neck to the left, which was the side that had hurt him.

He said, "Son of Bitch, you did not do anything!"

I asked him how his neck felt. He said his neck was just fine, but added, "You did not do anything." He did not understand what had just happened to him. The muscle group reset itself and released the contention that had caused the pain. He kept repeating, "Son of a bitch."

I thanked him for letting me help and sat back down at my desk.

Now setting your intention is everything in a massage. If your intention is to help someone fix themselves through massage, then you will be successful. Massage people do not prescribe medication, and we do not cure anyone. Massage people work with our clients' bodies to help their bodies self-fix. Ego has no place in healing—and I struggle the most with this issue. I have a big ego and when I do something, I want to be proud of it. I felt proud that I helped my coworker, but what I should have felt is happiness he no longer felt pain.

I have to constantly remind myself that it is not about me; it is about the person whom I am trying to help. I am supposed to facilitate care for people who want to work with me. If they are not willing, it is no use working with them, because there is no intention there. Put another way, you can lead a horse to water, but you cannot make it drink. I do not know how many times my father said that to me while I was growing up. By the way, I was the horse he was talking about.

MASSAGE FUNDAMENTALS

The time had finally come—and it was about time. In March 2018 and with 160 hours into my 500-hour Certified Massage Therapy program, I felt ready to do some actual massage. I had enjoyed taking the other classes like Acupressure, Energy Balancing, Ortho-Bionomy, and Reflexology. I had met some really interesting people in those classes. I have learned a lot. Much of that learning would be reinforced once I finished the Massage Fundamentals classes.

My Massage Fundamentals started in March and lasted six weekends. This was a very long set of classes—96 hours to be exact and all of those 96 hours were in the classroom. The classes consist of the A-Z of what happens in a massage session. This also includes classes on ethics, anatomy, and business. I balked at the ethics class because I was a philosophy major for most of my college career. I openly asked myself what an eight-hour ethics massage class could teach me about ethics? I very quickly checked myself on my attitude because I had to take the class to gain the hours. There was no testing out of a massage class. It was the cost of doing business and that was that. I just needed to do what I needed to do to get that piece of paper with 500 hours on it.

I excitedly began the Massage Fundamentals. Class began the normal way with students sitting in a circle and introducing ourselves. When it came my time to talk I went a little overboard about my plans after the class and what I had done previously. This introduction just came out of me. I had talked too much when I realized halfway through it I had gone over the top. It was too late, the old Scott had already spoken. It didn't feel right that I had gone overboard in this group. We had 17 people in the fundamentals class from pretty diverse backgrounds.

After everyone finished their introductions, we were handed our massage school binders that we were to bring to class each day. The binder included a list of definitions, legal information, and a loose listing that described our activities in the different classes. We referenced the binder for most of the classes, but we started to move away from it toward the end of the six weekends. Toward the end of the classes, we were already on our way to becoming massage therapists. The instructors allowed us to work on what we wanted to work on.

We first learned how to put up and take down a massage table. This seems like an easy thing to do, but it's not. There is a technique to it. I decided to start the class in the elevated back of the classroom on a slippery floor. The upper area in the classroom had an industrial laminate floor that made working with massage tables a little tricking. I learned pretty quickly that I did it all wrong. I looked around the room for some advice. Some of the students were actual massage professionals from other states. California changed its laws on massage and people from other states were unfairly having their training hours stripped from them and made to start over. After watching a few of the pros put up their tables, I quickly figured out who knew what they were doing and followed their lead. Table is up and in its upright position.

We learned basic draping or decent covering of the body and what to do and not to do. I had a lot of "do not dos" in this class. I am dyslexic, ADD, and I am left-handed. This is never considered "the-best-of-many-worlds" solution for anything. I am always backwards or flipping things around. All instructions were given from the right-handed perspective. I needed to translate in real-time. Normally, this is not an issue because I have been doing this all my life.

As a lefty, you are always in the minority—and right-handed people are in a fog about this issue, as they never have to deal with it. I had a bit of a problem with the instructors saying use your "right" hand and move it this way. I also had a habit of standing on the wrong side of the table because of the left-handed nature of my massage work. I led with my left, and I needed to let my ambidextrous ability out. In the beginning, I was a hot mess but I eventually got better.

I quickly learned that there was not enough room in the training area to have two beginning massage students working back to back. In later classes, this would not be an issue, because we were all aware of our surroundings. Massage students are not generally efficient with their body movements and positioning, so I constantly ran into other students. I also started out as a draping failure until I graduated out of the fundamentals class.

When left on my own, there is no problem. I am driving the massage ship and concentrating my intention toward my client.

Following instructor directions, I did not know the next step the instructor wanted me to do. I also worked too fast and too hard. I had no flow to my actions, and most of the modalities in massage need good flow to be relaxing. I just kept remembering all of those sports massages from when I raced bikes. I am a six-foot guy at 200 pounds. I have the ability to push really hard on someone. I needed to learn that not everyone wanted a firm grip or an elbow. After a while and some good coaching from students and instructors, I got the hang of it and the touch or feel of my massage matched what my clients expected. In fact, my fellow students started to request me as their partner and that felt good. To be accepted by one's peers is always a good thing.

My touch and flow got better and better. To be honest, no one in my Massage Fundamentals class gave a terrible massage. They were all really good, and that is a testament to the instructors and how hard the students worked. I always worried about choosing partners and doing something that would build a barrier between us. I decided before the massage classes ever started that I would take a backseat to other students' needs.

I made this decision because I had tired of the ego-driven-me-first attitude that I had before I started my two-year journey. I had gray hair and the other students did not, which meant a generational gap. It didn't matter though. We all joked about all kinds of things, and no one in that series of classes got butthurt over anything. I tried to not let anything stress me out. I think I accomplished this goal over time. I was going to massage school to help others, so it wasn't about me in the long run. I had to get with the program. I also wanted to make sure everyone felt welcome to work with me.

Most of the people who started the Massage Fundamentals class graduated. A few dropped off the radar because of life issues or because massage turned out to not be their thing. The series of fundamentals classes really did reach me. I got better at massage, increased my movement and flow, and my massage partners started to fall asleep on my table. There is no better compliment than having someone so comfortable with you working on them that they fall asleep. I grew a lot through that series of classes and felt even more confident in helping others. I also noticeably gained a calmness and ease of emotional tension by completing those classes. Good time—and time well spent.

I finally made it to the magic number of 500 hours in my massage training. When you reach the 500-hour mark everyone in the class applauds your effort and commitment. When the certificates are handed out at the end of the class, everyone congratulates you, and you feel like those 500 hours were 500 pounds you had been carrying around for the last year. It took almost a complete year of training to make it to 500 hours. I felt like I had accomplished something and it truly changed me. This achievement wasn't like my other accomplishments like getting my master's degree or winning bike races. I earned this accomplishment through time and commitment to a higher goal. Others noticed this change too. They voted me the most changed person out of that graduating class. This was not an official school thing; it was voted on by the people in that round of graduating class. Everyone clearly understood I would do massage to help others. I did have a couple of hurdles to overcome before I could petition to get my Certified Massage Therapist certificate.

MBLEX, RITE OF PASSAGE

The dreaded Massage and Bodywork Licensing Examination (MBlex) haunted me. To get a Certified Massage Therapist certificate you need to have 500 hours of massage training from an accredited massage school. This training is also broken up into several specific categories. You need to pass a live-scan security check, background check from the Department of Justice (DOJ) and the Federal Bureau of Investigation (FBI), and be fingerprinted. I left one thing out though. You also have to take the most dreaded test for a massage therapist, the MBlex.

The Mblex, an adaptive exam, is taken in a testing center under very heavy security to ensure that you are knowledgeable about the inner workings of the human body. It is an adaptive exam that has many different components to it. The Mblex's design makes you feel like you fail the exam the whole time you take it. I am well versed in these types of exams because, in the past, I have been certified by Microsoft, Cisco, and Citrix. For massage people, who do not have my experience, this test just blows them out of the water with anxiety, sleepless nights, and a lot of over-studying.

I agree that a professional exam should be passed before you work on people, but this test goes over the top. There is a huge difference in knowing what or how to give a massage and the information included in this exam. The exam does not test how well you do massage, it only tests your understanding of specific knowledge areas.

The MBlex is a pass/fail test with no score given to the test-taker. Mblex uses this approach to prevent employers from using test scores as a criterion in their hiring practices. The exam tests the knowledge of massage professionals. It is considered a starting point for what a massage professional should know.

The testing centers have rigid practices. It's frowned upon to even joke with the front-desk person. I felt this made them intentionally dispassionate. The exam is set up in a way that when you take it and answer correctly, it brings back a harder next question. The more answers you get correct the harder the exam gets.

When I took the exam in October 2018, I never felt comfortable, but I did do everything possible to help myself be successful. During the exam, I used my body as my own visual aid. When I got an anatomy question, I found the muscle on myself and worked the range of motion to see what else moved. I also looked at the source and the origin of the muscles or groups of muscles. I am sure it looked pretty funny watching me in the testing room.

The exam room, an angled room, had a proctor (testing observer) sit in a soundproof booth behind all the test-takers. I figured the test observer probably laughed at me because on anatomy questions I located the muscle on my body and rotated or flexed it to see which muscle acted as the aggressor, synergist, or agitator. I sat in the testing chair and contorted my body. I stuck my fingers between muscles to isolate the different ones. I know when I got to the gluteus maximus, I poked my butt and rotated my legs, which I am sure made quite a sight. Hey, I did what I needed to do to pass the exam and prove I had the required knowledge to become a Certified Massage Therapist.

After you finish the exam, you let the test observer know that you are done and take your pencil and piece of paper away from the exam desk. Once out of the exam area, I proceeded to the exam observer's desk to pick up my exam score. They turned over the exam score so no one could see any pass/fail status. I turned over the exam and saw that I had passed. Time to pop the champagne.

Many of my graduating class from massage school took the exam and passed it. Some were not so lucky. The ones who did not pass the MBlex all stated that they got frustrated with the exam and felt like they already failed it. What makes the exam so difficult is the number of topics the exam pulls from. Yes, you need to know your anatomy and pathology, but the way the questions are asked is deceiving. I had 96 hours of anatomy. I studied really hard for the test yet some of the questions still had me asking, "They are asking what?" In the end, I passed the dreaded MBlex. I passed it on my first try and completed this rite of passage.

ATRIAL FIBRILLATION (AFIB)

Just when things were going really well with massage school, my meditation practice, and my life in general, I had a huge setback. The setback is a long-term setback that I am still dealing with today—and it put limitations on what I can and cannot do. In January 2018 I had my first occurrence of Atrial Fibrillation (AFIB). As part of this journey, I am constantly reminded that the universe has lessons for me to learn. Some of those lessons are more enjoyable than others, and this one I considered a negative lesson. There have been a lot of lessons to learn, but life is never a straight line.

I saw AFIB as a curveball because it came out of nowhere; and in my opinion, a doctor's carelessness caused it. As I move forward on my journey, there are always going to be setbacks in life. AFIB is one of them. AFIB, a disorganization of electrical signals in the top chambers of the heart, causes erratic heartbeats. My first case came out of the blue, but the cardiologist most likely caused it by taking me cold turkey off a potassium-based blood pressure medication.

A few days earlier I had an office visit with my cardiologist. I showed signs of low blood pressure. The doctor worried that my blood pressure would become too low and I would start to have problems with my kidneys. My doctor did not believe me when he asked if I had taken any new medications or had been working out more. I told him, no, I wasn't taking new meds and I had been a couch potato ever since I had been diagnosed with an aortic aneurysm.

I did tell him I had started a meditation practice. I had been working with a therapist to better my personal life and mental well being. I let him know that I had made huge progress. I felt happy that it was having a positive effect on me. Later on that night, I received a voicemail from my doctor telling me to stop taking my blood pressure medication, and even though I was taking the maximum dosage of that medication, I should stop taking it immediately. Two days later I found myself in the emergency room.

After not taking my medication for a couple of days, I started feeling terrible. I didn't feel tired or even nauseous, but rather I just felt off. I tried to not let it bother me since I did not think it was a big deal. I thought it was just side effects of going off my blood pressure medicine. One evening I sat down with my wife on the couch for an informal dinner and watched the nightly news. After dinner I went to take my plates back into the kitchen. When I stood up, I knew something was wrong. I have always had the ability to feel my heartbeat—it is a conscious part of me. When I stood up, I could feel my heart skipping beats and my pulse increased way too rapidly.

I looked over at my wife and told her I was in trouble. My heart beated erratically. I felt like I was going to throw up. I decided to drive into work and walk into my hospital's ER. Since I did not feel any pain in my chest I felt safe to drive.

On the drive to the hospital, my heart rate got faster and faster, but I drove very calmly and smoothly. I am an endurance race-car driver, and I could have driven a lot faster but my heart would have been taking a good hit of adrenaline. In racing fast is slow. I know that sounds funny but it's really true. When you try to rush things, you overreact or over-correct. This is where mistakes happen. When you drive smoothly, you end up being faster in the end because everything is under control. You don't make driving mistakes that could take you out or damage the car. The increased heart rate started to get my attention when it hit 120 beats per minute. I knew I had a strong heart—120 beats per minute is not even close to my target workout range, so I kept calm and did not let myself overreact.

I arrived at the hospital. I found a parking place in the emergency room parking lot. This never happens because parking around the hospital is always difficult. I walked into the ER and stopped at the security screener. Security quickly moved me forward when I pointed to my heart and said I was having issues. He motioned me to the next desk to be checked in. I walked up to the desk, and when the attendant asked why I was there, I just looked at him and said that I had an erratic heartbeat. He stared at me and motioned for me to sit down and wait for the next medical tech. He did not believe me. I waited for five minutes, which was not bad for our ER. The medical tech called me up and I walked over to him. He sat behind a screened-in area for patient privacy. He too did not believe me until he took my pulse. I was up to 151 beats per minute. I looked at him and asked "EKG?" He quickly got me into a treatment room. I assisted him by pulling up my shirt to get the ball moving. Yes, I was in AFIB in a big way. I moved almost instantly from the treatment room to an ER bed where they hooked up both of my arms with IVs.

In hindsight, that was not a good move on my part—later on I would come to regret it. Since I had IVs in both arms, I could not bend my arms. I had to keep them semi-straight. This caused a lot of problems when I tried to sleep or eat. So the ports were in my arms; fluids were being pumped into me; and people moved around me with a purpose. I started to get a little concerned as people came and went, stating that they were there to take care of me. I had been pretty chill about the whole thing up until this point. I knew I had a strong heart. I didn't feel any chest pain. I had several vials of blood drawn that resulted in a battery of tests. I started to feel like a pincushion. I found out too late that the lab could not use a port to draw blood, and I had two ports already in the veins that they nicknamed the "Highways". The lab techs needed to find other veins to pull blood from, and they were not being gentle about it.

After the tests came back they found some deficiencies in my blood work. They decided to admit me to the hospital. My heart had not slowed down. Here is where things got tricky. I had not planned on nor did I want to stay overnight in the hospital. I did not understand the severity of my situation. No one around me would explain it to me in a way I could understand. I texted my wife, who did not make the trip to the hospital with me, and my boss. I let them know that I was being admitted to the hospital—and I had not planned for it.

The tricky part about being admitted was that they requested a cardiologist to work with me. The on-duty cardiologist turned out to be the same guy who had diagnosed me earlier with lung cancer. I stated very clearly that I wanted him nowhere near me. I had parted ways with him for being incompetent. I decided that working with the ER doctors would be best for now. I would see my cardiologist in the morning after he had done his hospital rounds. I agreed to this approach since the ER doctors discussed my treatment plan with me, and it made sense at the time. The ER doctors told me that they were going to use medication to slow my heart down and my heart would reset to normal rhythm over time. It was a form of rhythm control for my heart.

The doctor could not tell me how long it would take to correct my rhythm, but he hinted that by this time tomorrow, I should be fine. Now we had a plan. They increased the rhythm-control medication per the treatment plan. I had a long night ahead of me. Since I had ports in both arms I could not bend my arms or roll on my side to sleep. I felt terribly uncomfortable, but I had allowed them to do it to me, so I couldn't blame anyone but myself for that one.

After 24 hours my treatment plan hadn't worked, but my heart did slow to the point of one-plus seconds between beats. In fact, my heart had slowed so much that they had to discontinue the use of the rhythm-control drug. Yet my heart rhythm still wasn't right. I was still in AFIB. The medications that they gave me made me feel worse. It felt like someone sat on my chest. I described it as a narrowing of my airway and a 20-pound weight on my upper chest. I could live with it in the grand scheme of things; however, I had to work at breathing, which isn't fun. The situation began to drag on me. I started to get a little cranky because nothing had worked the way it should.

My current cardiologist met with me in the hospital room and stated that I needed to stay on the medications for as long as it took to get the rhythm corrected. He said he was sorry that I was in the hospital with AFIB, but he did not know why this happened to me. I suggested the removal of my maximum dosage blood pressure medication caused the problem. To back it up, I referred to my blood workup, which showed I had low potassium. My blood pressure medication was made of potassium. The doctor would not have any part of my theory about what had put me in the hospital. He told me to stay on the existing treatment plan.

This conversation started to cause a bit of friction between my doctor and me. I wouldn't let him off the hook that easily. I have never respected people who cannot at least admit there is a chance that they made an error. Yes, doctors get sued, I understand this, but he made the decision to remove the blood pressure medication—and he had to own it by himself.

After the meeting with my doctor, the nurses started acting differently. Each shift the nurses asked a series of questions about alcohol consumption. My wife and I both separately told the doctor the same thing. We had not consumed any alcohol in six days.

The fun began when my immediate family started to circle the wagons around me. They were all there at the hospital. I started to be very insistent that I wanted a different treatment plan. It had been better than 48 hours and no resolution. I needed to take charge of the situation. My mom always taught me that you are responsible for your own well being. You cannot farm out that responsibility to someone else.

My wife and I had done our Advanced Medical Directives before the beginning of the new year, and it was on file with the hospital. I finally had it with the hospital and their insistence that drinking alcohol had caused the problem that put me in the hospital and the failure of their treatment plan to work. Changes were in order. I felt tired and cranky by this time, so I got labeled a "Problem Patient".

What I wanted now was to be manually cardio inverted. In English, I wanted them to use the electric paddles on me and shock me back to the correct rhythm. I told them I wanted them to crank up "Old Sparky" and let me have it. They attempted to tell me that if we stayed on the treatment plan it would work eventually. They could not tell me how much longer it would take to convert with the drug cocktail, so I once again

demanded a change in my treatment plan. They finally agreed
to my request and rounded up a doctor to do the procedure. My
current cardiologist was busy with office appointments, and I
didn't want to wait for him. He had pissed me off, and I just
wanted to be done with this situation. Patience does not run in
my family.

They did finally agree to the procedure. I chomped at the bit to
be cardio inverted. The nurses all made comments to me about
being so happy about getting shocked. They thought I should be
afraid of it, which I was not. I looked forward to it. I am not the
first person who needed this done and I would not be the last.
Just as in skydiving, the first step is a big step and you cannot
fly back into the plane after jumping out of it. Make the decision
and move forward with it.

I was very clear in my mind about what I wanted and nothing
would stop me from getting the hell out of that hospital. I
was already ready when the nurses came into my room. I was
prepared with a pen in my hand and in the signing position
even though I had the ports in both arms. It hurt but I needed to
sign the paperwork to get this done. What they had been doing
didn't work. I wanted to take control of the situation for my
betterment. I signed the documents and waited to be taken down
to the post-operation area. This area had been selected for its
space. All the people waited for me except the doctor.

I was impressed by the staff in the postoperative area at the
hospital, as they were all business and they understood that I

was there for a reason. Without the doctor present, they did the equivalent of a Skydiving Dirt Dive, which is a run-through of all the positions you will be taking during the skydive. I felt happy to see this approach. I would be able to see what they would be doing to me. They also verbally explained everything much to my relief. I remember warmly smiling at them. I felt like I was amongst friends. They would take care of me.

The doctor arrived 30 minutes late. I didn't need to show my disdain for him being late. All the nurses let him have it in their own special nurse way. The cardiologist introduced himself, and I got a good, positive vibe from him. He explained what he was going to do and why he was going to do it. He told me that I would be put under. They would adhere the electro-shock pads to me and then weigh me down with sandbags. He asked me if I had any questions and I remember saying to him, "Light me up."

I got a good look at the elector pads. The pads were bigger than I expected, and the electrical leads on them were as big as power cables for your car battery. The nurses saw that I looked at them. They became concerned that I might be getting scared. I just smiled. I settled into the hospital bed. I didn't care what they thought. Then the doctor gave the order to give me the sedative. I waved to the staff as I went under.

They electro cardio inverted me once and I went back into normal rhythm. I woke up in my room with my close family in attendance. I wanted to be discharged. This is when my parents stepped in and told me to cool my jets. I needed to let the drugs in my system dissipate before Sandra, my wife, could drive me home. They wanted me to stay in bed to make sure my heart did not go back into AFIB. After some time passed, I became excited when I got the final okay to leave. We jailbroke from the hospital and did not look back.

Now I look back at my experience with more educated eyes. I would have done things differently than they were done at my hospital. Since that first episode I have ended up in the ER on multiple occasions. I have learned to look differently at AFIB. It was clear that I needed to change doctors. I found in my exit paperwork the doctor's notes stated that I had consumed alcohol three days prior to going into the ER. This note was a blatant lie—and I called the doctor on it. I contacted his office and let the receptionist know that the doctor had lied on my patient record and I wanted it corrected. When the receptionist objected, I told her I had proof that my medical record was falsified and I insisted that it be changed to what reality is, not what the doctor wanted it to be. I also insisted that I have a right to have that medical record corrected. I wouldn't let the doctor get away with this duplicity. I made him correct the medical record, but not before he threatened me that if I made him correct the error, that he would fire me as a patient. I already planned on getting a new cardiologist, so I insisted that he correct his error. I also do not take threats easily, and I think it was completely unnecessary to do so. This was a chump move. I wanted to put the proverbial pie in the doctor's face.

I am not a litigious type of person. I didn't plan to sue the doctor. I couldn't 100 percent prove that the AFIB was a direct result of taking me off my potassium-based blood pressure medicine. Do I believe that it is true? Yes I do, but proving it wasn't worth my time. He owns it, and he knows it. He did make the corrections to my medical record. I also decided that I would go to another hospital closer to my house the next time I went into AFIB.

The takeaway from this ordeal is that my new cardiologist diagnosed me with "Random AFIB". Since that time I have been in the ER twice. I now know the signs and have a way of dealing with AFIB that self-corrects. I bought an electrocardiogram or EKG machine called Kardia. The Kardia app works off my cell phone. I know when AFIB ramps up. I know at what heart rate to take rhythm-correcting medication. The new hospital learned from my other hospital what not to do. They came up with a drug cocktail that works for me. Let's call it a trial-and-error win for me. This new treatment keeps me out of the hospital ER. I am also in control of my treatment plan and my own destiny. No being admitted to the hospital, no electro-shocking, and no cranky patient, nurses, and doctors. This gave me some peace of mind, because spending several days in the hospital is not something I am into doing.

NANCY

Since I had to come to grips with my AFIB diagnosis, I decided that I needed to talk to someone again. I have had really good luck just talking to people. It's not a crutch but a way of dealing with difficulties. All the changes happening to and around me made me look to another therapist's perspective.

I met with Nancy at her temporary office in Sacramento, Ca in June 2018. As with so many events during my journey, Nancy hosted a Meetup to try and build her new therapy business. The Meetup consisted of six people in a small room talking about their wants and needs, and their current problems. I went to the Meetup because Nancy worked with athletes. I thought a Meetup was a good way to introduce myself and get a feel for how she works.

The Meetup members all confessed to never having talked to a therapist and gave Nancy a general list of wants and needs. Their wants and needs were pretty common in nature. They all involved things like dealing with money issues, being attractive to members of the opposite sex, and getting along with others. I was the only outlier in the group—and I pretty much expected that to be the case. I had moved further down the road toward change than most people. I am not being judgemental—it is what it is.

I wanted to talk about my AFIB and what it meant for me and my life. I also wanted to discuss issues related to my blood-pressure problems. When it came time for me to speak about my issues I just talked in generalities. I did not need to go into specifics with the group, as I got a good feeling for what Nancy was about. I became a wallflower for the rest of the Meetup. I decided to reach out to Nancy later on that week to set up a session.

The meeting resulted in me prepaying for six therapy sessions. Nancy had just started her therapy practice and needed to get some cash flow going. I agreed to this because I liked her style. I also thought she could take me to the finish line of my journey. The sessions with Nancy were based on where I was at on my journey and what both of us felt about it. This was again not a normal therapist-client setup or along the lines of what I had done with Samantha and Lynn. I wanted to know Nancy's opinion on things. She wasn't shy about telling me what she thought and why she thought it. Again, I didn't need validation; I looked to Nancy as a sounding board.

Nancy had just finished up her master's degree in Psychology, which gave her flexibility in her approach. I found this attractive. She willingly avoided putting me in a box or attempting to co-op me into a process. I know that Samantha's process worked very well, but the further I got into talking with people the more I wanted this process to be more freestyle than formal. Nancy also had a great way of swinging my personality pendulum back the other way. I had been overcompensating and overly downplaying my past accomplishments. I know this change had been the goal, but it had gone too far. It got to the point where I wasn't being my true self, which had gotten to me a bit. I had finally toned myself down *too* much. She insisted on putting a little kick-ass back into me.

Nancy is a tall woman at around 6' with semi-long, black hair. She is also built like a fitness model. She has square shoulders and a presence about her. She earned those square shoulders as a gymnast and that information came out in the initial meeting with me. The therapist doesn't traditionally talk about themselves. I wanted to get to know her personally before I opened up. She proved to me that she was aware of how I felt and the depth of some of my losses. She is equally as no-nonsense as Samantha, except you can imagine Nancy putting her iron fist in a velvet glove.

Nancy actively uses Neuro-Linguistic Programming (NLP) in her sessions. NLP, a grouping of communication techniques, works well with emotional and trust issues. We used NLP to get a foundational trust built and to explore how I felt about things. I felt excited about doing some of the NLP exercises. I had already studied NLP. I took my NLP class online where I watched a demonstration, which is a lot different than actually going through the exercises in person. Just like in Reiki, if I was going to use NLP in the future, I would retake the classes in person—and thus, there would be no faking or taking the easy way out. I was honestly more interested in the content of NLP then actually doing it as a profession.

In one session Nancy and I did a visualization to help me with communication issues. We took an interaction I had with a co-worker and made it pivot 90 degrees. I watched myself in an interaction and observed what I did during the interaction. I have always found this to be valuable. When you watch yourself in an interaction and actually see in your mind how that interaction worked out it gives it clarity. In my case, the interaction did not work out well.

We had interacted about a network project that I had been working on at the hospital. I had a heavy discussion with the project's stakeholder. He didn't seem to want to help make his project a success. I had a history with this stakeholder, too. I always had to push to get anything done with him.

When I interacted with him, I had not been being present. The problem, in my opinion, related to our past history. I had pretty aggressive body language, which put the stakeholder into a defensive posture. I clearly had not been listening to him. I had already decided what I was going to say in response to him instead of patiently waiting for him to finish talking.

This is a classic example of how *not* to communicate with someone. Even though I had some history with this person I should respect him enough to listen. This visualization told me about my behavior. It wasn't the first time I had noticed this trait in myself. Samantha used to catch me doing this type of communication—and she would call me out on it. She did it with respect even though she had put that 12-pound sledgehammer to the side of my head. Now here came the sledgehammer again. I had not learned my lesson yet. I repeated history with the project stakeholder. I needed to actively listen to him and not try to win the argument.

Takeaway number one, I didn't respect the other person enough to listen to him. I came up with my rebuttal or attack instead of waiting for him to finish his thought. I broke off the exercise and just looked at Nancy and told her I needed to think about what I just saw. Nancy knew what had happened in the visualization since I had verbalized it while I saw the mental picture. I knew I was wrong. I cannot speak for the other person's actions in the interaction, but I can correct my actions. Plus, perception is such a tricky thing. I also recognized that I had relived bad past project experiences with the project's stakeholder. I had jumped to conclusions that he would flake like he had done in the past on another project. It was a perception problem. I needed to work on myself before I could work with others.

At the next meeting with Nancy, we decided that we should look at the reason I had high blood pressure and try and do something about it. High blood pressure runs in my family, so it is not surprising I have it, but there are other factors to consider. Diet, sleep, exercise, relationships, and job stress all play a factor in high blood pressure. Also, family attitude plays a part. My family traditionally has a lot of behaviors that can lead to high blood pressure. I come from a family of doers, not passive individuals; so we all push a bit too hard at times. My similar attitude contributed to the problem. I felt convinced that if I mellowed out a bit and stopped trying to control things, I might be able to lower my blood pressure.

We started with a visualization to lower my blood pressure. Nancy began by having me go into a deeply relaxed state. Once I relaxed Nancy had me visualize a long hallway with different colored doors along the sides. She asked me to imagine a doorway at the very end of the hallway and to approach it while noticing the other doors as I walked by them. Once I got to the end of the hallway, she asked me to describe the door. I described the door as a solid-wooden door painted white with an antique door handle. The doorknob, an oblong and brass one, felt wiggly when I turned it. I turned the doorknob and let myself into the room.

I was pretty deep in the visualization and in a relaxed state related to a lot of "flow" and fine details. Flow means everything happened with every instruction from Nancy. I verbalized everything that happened without hesitation or questioning the requests coming from Nancy. It became a very surreal experience. She asked me to describe the room as I entered it. The room was a little larger than 10' x 10', which would be the size of a standard bedroom. The walls were covered in a magenta wallpaper, and the wallpaper had some texture to it.

As I entered the room, Nancy asked me to locate a dial on the far wall and tell her once I had found it. I did find the dial. I described it as a dial that was about a foot around in the middle of the wall. I did not understand why the dial was a foot around, but I guess I saw high blood pressure as a big problem. Big problems get big dials. Nancy told me to walk up to the dial and turn the dial to lower my blood pressure. For safety reasons, I did not turn the dial all the way down, I turned it halfway down. I didn't turn it all the way down since I did not know the end result of the adjustment with my subconscious mind. I have found that I am subject to the power of suggestion. Why over do it when we could do this visualization again.

I did not want to lower my blood pressure too low—although in hindsight that would be an easier problem to deal with because of my aortic aneurysm. Nancy now wanted me to exit the room walking backwards. I did not question why it needed to be backwards; I just did it and closed the door upon exit. Now back in the hallway, I looked back at my starting point for the visualization. I thought this was going to be the end of the visualization, but it was not.

Nancy asked me if there was anything in the hallway that interested me. As I walked down the hallway, I noticed a yellow door, which caught my attention for some reason. Nancy wanted me to explore the yellow door. She had me walk up to the door. When I arrived at the door, she asked me to describe it. The door was a different type of solid-wood door painted yellow. The door handle looked different and more modern-looking. This door handle appeared more like a lever. It had a brushed-metal surface on the handle. The handle reminded me of something you would see in Europe. It had a very clean, minimalist design. Nancy instructed me to open the door. I turned the door handle, but I could not enter the room. Something in the room stopped me from going in. The door would only open a smidge, and I could see just slightly into the room. I noticed that the room was painted purple, but I could not see anything else.

Since I could not open the door, we decided to change up the visualization a bit. Nancy wanted me to visualize myself on the other side of the door and to see what happens. I followed instructions. I felt very surprised at the result. Yes, I imagined or saw myself on the other side of the door. I only saw black before I got instantly put back in the hallway. I tried this several times, but I always got put back in the hallway. Nancy and I were baffled about what had happened. Neither of us had ever experienced anything like it.

We were perplexed since I could give the smallest detail about the blood pressure room, the door handles, and color and textures of the rooms, but still could not open the yellow door. This yellow door had different qualities, and I could see them, but no matter what I did, nothing allowed me to enter the room. Nancy became convinced I had some sort of mental block related to this room. We needed to let some time go by before attempting to do the visualization again. I slowly came out of the visualization. I felt very groggy and wanted to take a nap. This feeling faded over time as I came clear of the visualization and started to feel normal again.

In a later session, we decided that we would not do the visualization again, because between our sessions I figured out what had been happening. When I say "figured it out," I had a hunch because of a dream. I normally cannot exactly remember dreams, but to me the yellow door represented the future. By only being able to open the door a little and being put back into the hallway I was being sent a clear message. I needed to live in and stay in the present. The universe had talked to me and I listened.

My thoughts on the realization that the yellow door was the future and to not worry about the future until it gets here, were confirmed by another dream. I know this sounds like it is out there a bit, but I realized you find what you are looking for by *looking* for it. I searched for the meaning of why these things were happening in my mind (this is like Occam's razor). "Entities should not be multiplied unnecessarily." Put in my language "keep it simple stupid." The KISS method is one of my favorite ways of cutting through an overly complicated situation and getting down to what is important.

I normally do not remember dreams in their entirety. The dreams that have an impact are the ones that come and are very vivid. The dream occurred in March, and I started to document my dreams after this one. I thought my subconscious had been talking to me. I needed to continue to listen. If I could learn something through these dreams and not have to learn a lesson the hard way, I was very interested.

The dream started with me entering an elevator. The elevator was a semi-modern elevator with thin, steel plate walls. While

I was in the elevator the doors got stuck halfway closed and wouldn't fully close. The elevator doors finally started to move after I started pushing and pulling on them. I did not understand why the doors got stuck, and all of a sudden the doors released and started to close.

I backed away from the doors to the back of the elevator. I began to have a notion of fear and questioning, as I felt confused by the doors' action. As the doors were in the process of closing, the doors came off the guiderails at an angle of 15 degrees and with the inner side of the doors pointing in. I did not ask myself how I knew it was 15 degrees but the walls angled in. I was being squeezed to the back of the elevator, as the elevator unexpectedly fell. I did not fight the elevator doors or attempt to escape from the elevator. The elevator crashed to the ground and the doors crushed me. I was dead as the result of being crushed and then I woke up from the dream sweating with a very rapid heartbeat.

I know my subconscious worked overtime now. The symbolism for me was you must die to be reborn. One could say that this was a rising-of-the-Phoenix moment for me. I did not fight for my life, which was the old me. The old me would fight to the end and not rest until it was over. I have stared death in the face like when I went skydiving, rock climbing, car racing, and white-water kayaking. I am personally amazed that I lived through some of my escapades, but I did—and I did because I always fought to the end and didn't stop until it ended.

VOLUNTEERING

I have always thought that volunteering was an important thing to do if you have the ability to do it. My mother and father have always volunteered to help their community or someone in need. My family did not think of volunteering as a conscious action to look good—they were in the position to do it and had the ability to help.

My mom was the President of the National Parent Teacher Association (PTA) in Davis, Ca., served on the School Board, and helped write bonds to build several schools and a local hospital. She also was one of the people to bring Suicide Prevention to Yolo County. My father always worked with the engineering community to better the engineering standards and how things are designed. My father for many years was President of the American Council of Engineering Companies (ACEC).

I have asked myself several times over the two-year journey what was important to me and how I could help? It did not take long to become aware of a soulful response. *I want to help others be as successful as they can be just like people did for me.* This became my new mantra. I want more people to have the ability to think about something they want to do and execute on it. I want more people to have the confidence of thinking, "I think, therefore I do." I had a lot of thoughtful people pour time and money into me to give me the opportunity to be successful. I think I did a pretty good job of doing just that, and now it was my time to help others be successful with their goals and do what I could to help. Now I always viewed volunteering as a selfless act. I truly want others to find their success and feel the pride from others' successes.

So, how can I do this? During my journey, I have tried several things and some of them have worked better than others. In the next couple of chapters I will explain some of the volunteering I did during my two-year journey.

MASSAGE

In late March of 2018, after I finished with my Massage Fundamentals class I saw a volunteer request posting on the job board at my massage school. This organization looked for people to volunteer at events like marathons and ultra marathons. This group has been volunteering at events like this for years. I wanted to be part of this volunteer effort since this would help me with my eventual goal of working with athletes. I had the time and ability to help, why not volunteer? I wanted to get a hold of the organization's owner and let him know I wanted to volunteer. I felt cautious and a little intimidated by the whole process. I did not have a lot of massage experience working on people outside of the classroom—and I would be working on very successful people.

It took me a week or so of procrastination before I got the nerve to email the owner, letting him know that I existed and that I wanted to meet with him about volunteering. The owner nicely got back to me in a couple of days after receiving my email. I set up a date and time with the owner to go over what is involved in volunteering and how their program works. I wanted to make sure that the people and I clicked and we all got along. I did not want to volunteer and then find that the organization was a train wreck. In the initial email to the owner I asked him, "How does one work with you?" To my surprise, he replied,

"You volunteer."

I arrived at their offices on time for my appointment and I walked into the office. The building's exterior design is made of rustic wood painted red, which wasn't what I expected. I expected either a spa or medical-office-type setup. The office had a theme, a mix between New Mexico chic and California ghost town. The owner warmly greeted me as I walked in. The owner took me over to the picture wall of their customers. He and his staff have every reason to be proud of what they have built. All of his famous and not-so-famous clients were up on his wall. The group prides itself as a massage shop where there is a little pain in the gain. The ultra-marathon community just loves their staff and style. To me it makes sense for the runners, because sometimes you need to go deep to break up problem areas you develop doing extreme training.

The owner and I talked for about 30 minutes. We had a cordial and warm conversation about what would be expected of me and the different type of events they participated in. I got a very good vibe from him and I understood his quirkiness. I let him know that I wanted to volunteer if he would have me.

On the way out the door, the owner stopped me and asked me a really simple question: "Did we pass the interview?" I looked at him with no surprise and said, "Yes you all did." The owner knew very well I had been feeling him out and that I would not volunteer for just anyone. I wanted to be associated with the right crew for future volunteering. I also knew that they were plugged into the people and events that would allow me to serve others and do it in a bigger way than I could by myself. This was a double-win in my view.

A couple of weeks after the visit to their offices I juggled my schedule and signed up for 10 events. The first volunteer event took place at the American River 50-mile (AR50) ultramarathon. I looked forward to volunteering, but I felt very nervous about participating. I looked back on this and asked myself why I felt nervous? I would be working on athletes. How easy is that? It is like working on myself. Hindsight is always 20/20.

I wanted to arrive at the AR50 early because I did not want to get lost but yet I did. I ended up at the wrong Auburn Overlook Park. It became pretty obvious that I landed in the wrong place. I headed down into the Auburn Ravine toward the river and not to the top parking lot and park. It is called "Overlook" for a reason. My GPS did me wrong, which was not the first time my GPS had led me astray. I quickly did a Google search on my phone and found the right park. The Auburn Overlook Park has plenty of parking and enough room for vendors and food booths. The massage team had their easy-up tents set up close to the finish line, which enabled us to watch the runners and cheer them on.

I approached the massage team's tent area and saw that they had already had four massage tables set up. All the tables had disposable paper/plastic sheets on them, with disposable head-rest covers. Two elastic bands held down the table covering, which made it easy to change the coverings and headrest covers between clients. Since the runners cross the line and then perform their warm down, they don't take any time to clean up. They are full of mud, sweat, and poison oak. The poison oak concerned me. When I get poison oak it's bad. I once had it over 70 percent of my body. It's a terrible experience to get poison oak that bad. I would not wish it on anyone. I ended up in the ER pleading for help, as the poison oak advanced up my leg.

I thought the massage team's precautions made perfect sense. You can't have proper linens at this type of event. In-between runners being worked on, the massage team pulled the headrest and table cover off. Then we used sanitation wipes to clean the table. We also used surgical gloves to protect us from all contaminates. This way, we limited the runners and ourselves from being exposed to cross-contamination.

Four-hundred-plus runners participated in the race. We needed clean tables and a clean working area. It came time to go to work as the runners crossed the finish line. The owner asked me to observe how he works with the runners when they come in, and I paid close attention. I now acted as a reflection of his business, so this made sense that he would want me to work his way. After watching him work on one of the runners, he had me take the other side of the next runner we worked on. More and more runners finished now. The line started to stack up with people on the waitlist. We worked on a couple more runners when he asked me if I wanted to work solo. I looked at him and replied, "I have to earn my wings sometime, it might as well be now."

I quickly moved to another massage table and asked for the next runner. It only took two runners crossing my table before the owner walked over to me and put his hand on my shoulder. He told me that he had been watching me and I had done just fine. I was on my own for the rest of the day. I remember that I started to hum the song "Born Free". I don't know why, but everyone started to laugh at me when they heard it. I just pictured a dog running freely in a grassy field. I had been set free to help the runners and away I went with it.

It was a good thing that he had cut me loose. The waitlist got really long. We cleared the waitlist and kept the runners happy. It had been a long day volunteering at the AR50. I had been happy to break down the equipment at 8 PM. The other volunteers all told me I did a great job. At no time did any of the runners think I was a massage student. I worked like a pro and had a great time doing it. I had more than 20 runners come across my table that day. Massages averaged between 15 to 20 minutes each. Most were 15 minutes because of the long waitlist. I felt exhausted and headed home to take a shower. I did not eat dinner that night. I made it to my bed and face-planted into it.

SUICIDE PREVENTION

I have attempted over the years to become a crisis-call taker three times. I finally got the window of opportunity in July 2018 to take on that challenge. Sometimes when you volunteer, you do not fully understand the commitment level you have agreed to take on—and Suicide Prevention work required this kind of dedication. I say "fully understand" because being a crisis operator for Suicide Prevention is a big job. Until you get in and start doing it, you do not fully understand the commitment. This happened to me. This is the first organization that I have worked with that did not get what they paid for. I could not fulfill my commitment with them. A good reason stopped me from volunteering. My wife got promoted, which meant that she would be traveling more. Increased pay and responsibilities sometimes mean the family structure and commitments need to be re-evaluated. It was too bad because my family has been a supporter of Suicide Prevention since the early 1980s.

As I mentioned earlier in the book I had taken a run at suicide. I like to call myself a suicidal failure—and I am damn proud of it. It's a strange thing to be proud of. I believe the suicide attempt made me a stronger person. It also helped me deal with my cancer and aneurysm diagnosis. I developed the ability to take big hits and still keep pushing forward.

I think a lot of people who are part of Suicide Prevention have either tried to commit suicide or had someone close to them commit suicide. I started training with Suicide Prevention in early July of my two-year journey. I felt motivation to help others who were in deep pain to realize they can get themselves out of their crises. I had done this before when I was a college instructor. I had several people who suffered from PTSD, depression, or just had bad things happen to them. I either would notice the student not acting like themselves or the student would approach me with their problems. I can tell you some of my military students carried around a lot of dark memories that no one should have to go through. War is not fun or glorious, and for the most part, unnecessary. I am happy to report none of my students ever completed the act of suicide, but some came very close.

My suicide motivation came after my cycling career ended. I felt crushed—and I didn't know what to do with myself. I felt confused and angry, and my plans for my life had been upended. I attempted suicide with a fixed blade Buck knife that my dad had given to me. My saving grace was that the blade had a curve to it. When I went to end it all, the blade deflected and only cut into me a little. I felt shocked. I did not want to tell anyone I had attempted suicide. A couple of butterfly bandages took care of my wound and the shock of what I did actually pulled me out of my depression. It gave me a different perspective on life. It is just too bad that I felt like I needed to end myself to free myself.

It always amazes me how events like this one can pull or show you a different direction to go in life. At that moment of enacting my death, the end result showed me a different path that was worth exploring. The universe opens doors when you are willing to listen. In my case, it took me to almost end my life to see that there was not just one door; there were many doors where I could go to continue to live a productive life.

Being a crisis phone-line operator is not an easy job. Because of this, the Yolo County chapter of Suicide Prevention requires you to undergo a six-week intensive training with a lot of call simulations. These simulations were very intense and felt realistic. You were in the moment and you needed to think on your feet. For the most part I felt ok with the simulations. My biggest fear was to get a call from a student who was failing school because he or she were either not going to class or not handing in their assignments. My experience as a college instructor for six years kind of jaded me about these kinds of situations. My second fear would be a teenage pregnancy. I only had one call from a student failing school—and that was a test call. I find test calls cruel. I say this because when the phone rings your anxiety level goes way up. Someone on the other line is having a really bad day. I cannot go into detail about the calls I took, but from the start of training to my last phone call took around six months. Six months is just not enough time to volunteer, especially after they put so many hours into training me. I had been able to honor all of my commitments up until this point in my life. Suicide Prevention deserves public support. If you or someone you know is having problems, or you need some advice on how to help someone, please call the National Suicide Prevention Hotline at 1-800-273-8255.

THE THINGS I LEARNED ALONG MY JOURNEY

I learned a few things during my journey, but some were not as obvious as others. As I worked on myself first and then started to work on my relationships with others, I came across a few things that needed direct and immediate attention. In the following chapters, there are more details on things that came up during my journey. There is always some good with the bad. I had to be honest with myself about looking at different items. Change can sometimes be stressful, and things change quickly while you are under stress.

PUT YOUR PHONE DOWN

In the very beginning of my two-year journey, I hurt my relationships with people all around me. I started learning all these new NLP techniques, being present with people, and getting more attuned to what people felt. I learned I had not been fully present with people whether they stood in front of me or sat at the dinner table. It took my wife telling me that she did not want to go on vacation with me if I had my cell phone on me. This shocked me. I quickly realized that I had a real problem on my hands.

I had become addicted to my phone. I didn't realize what it had been doing to my relationship with my wife. I am an Ingress player, and Ingress had taken over my life. For those who do not play Ingress, it's a real-time, capture-the-flag-type game with teams. The game's main objective is to capture portals and link locations, and then build fields over opposing teams' portals. Portals are significant locations in the game. Ingress portals are interesting spots like plague locations, museums, odd signs, and just about anything intriguing. Ingress is an addicting game. The game rewards players with badges for things like the most fields, portal visits, and most hacks. I am a level 16 Ingress player, and it took me 663 days to get there. At present, there is no higher level in the game than level 16.

How did I get to level 16? I ignored everyone around me but other Ingress players. This problem obviously needed to be addressed. The goal or end game was to get to level 16 as quickly as possible. This meant playing on the way to work, at lunch with my co-workers, and after work on the way home. My player ID was Spiderman666. I got pretty good at the game. I had read the book *Sun Tzu's Art of War* and put his strategies to work. One of those strategies involved an exit plan—and that plan was to make it to level 16 and then semi-retire. Ingress had consumed my life. I wanted my life back after my wife's confession.

My wife suffered through trips to Washington DC, Vancouver BC, and Boston, MA. I would have my phone in my hand playing Ingress while walking around the different cities and hacking new portals and capturing other portals. My wife felt ignored, and I didn't blame her. I had to own this situation and put the phone down. One of the traits of my family is that we do not give up easily, and we sure as hell do not quit. This attitude had suited me well over the years. I was not about to start giving up and quitting at my age. My saving grace was to focus on the goal and get to level 16.

When I started my journey, I became aware that I wasn't being present with people. I realized that I never wanted to be *that* guy who stared at his phone in a restaurant while his wife or friends sat there and fumed. I didn't want to be *that* guy, who when he and his wife walked the dog every Saturday and Sunday paid more attention to hacking portals than being with his significant other and enjoying the walk together. With my wife's help, I put the phone down and realized what I had been missing for 663 days. I am happy this did not end my marriage, but I believe it came very close. I had become so driven to succeed at the game that I had missed the big picture right in front of me the whole time.

Weaning yourself off a cell phone/game addiction wasn't easy to do. I have a very compulsive personality. I did not go cold turkey. I started to leave my cell phone at home for walks with the dog or in the car when I went wine tasting. I also decided that I needed to not have my cell phone with me sometimes at work. I constantly looked at my phone during meetings. My Supervisor would text me and tell me to put my phone down and pay attention. My Supervisor also knew about the game's addictive qualities since he had rabidly played for a year or so.

My clean break came when I signed up for massage school. So many things that I wanted to change happened in that one year of massage school. I did not attack massage school like I did everything else. I intentionally decided to observe, listen, and then act or give an opinion. In massage school, they don't allow phones in the classroom. Phones got tucked away in your backpack. During break is when you could correspond with people or look at Facebook. During my 500-hour massage program, I got to the point where I would show up for class, check my email, and then turn the phone off for the day. I did not need to talk to anyone. My work knew when I went to class. They didn't give me any fallout about not taking a call.

I learned a much-needed lesson: *I did not need a phone with me.* I escaped from my digital leash and my obsession with Ingress. To this day, I have continued with this lesson. I intentionally leave my phone at my desk and only carry it when I know that I need it for an information technology project. I also decided that even though my cell phone could be a source for music, the phone would never be used in the massage room when I work with clients.

Putting my cell phone down and being present with people became one of the most important takeaways of my two-year journey. Yes, I have made some incredible personality changes in my life, but being present with someone is the most important thing. We are on this Earth for a finite period of time. Time is our most valuable asset to give to someone and you cannot take it back. I wish I would have learned this lesson earlier in my journey. I apologize to anyone I ignored because I had played Ingress.

SOMETIMES FRIENDS NEED TO GO

When a person starts to change and their friends do not, there is a conflict or relationship stress that occurs. You could consider this a "friction of change". Sometimes this conflict or stress escalates into moving on and out with a relationship or an understanding of what I call "change lag". In change lag, the friend works on change but takes a while before he or she enacts that change. This is kind of a catch-up phase. It is natural when this happens that you have a distance grow in the friendship. Sometimes you are closer and other times you are farther apart. It is very rare to find a friend who is on the same journey as you and you grow the relationship together.

We are in a constant state of change whether we want it or not. When you look at relationships you can only be 50 percent of one. This leads to some interesting thoughts because a 50/50 relationship can be looked upon as a kind of equilibrium. You attempt to keep that equilibrium while everything changes over time around you. If you put in over 50 percent in a relationship, you don't respect the other person's ability to own their 50 percent of it. If you are under 50 percent, you may not value the relationship as much as the other person does. This is a tricky concept that many books have covered.

I am part of a book club that meets once a month. We have read several books on relationships and how you should evaluate them. Although this concept is not new to me, Don Miguel Ruiz's *The Mastery of Love* gives great detail about how relationships must be balanced—or said another way, they must be a 50/50 split or it may not work in the long term. If you think about it, it makes perfect sense that you get what you put into a relationship. Once you try too hard or you look for excuses to not put in equal effort, it knocks the relationship off-balance, and this imbalance means the relationship doesn't work right.

Change is sometimes a stressful thing in relationships. It isn't easy to maintain a solid relationship when changes happen all at once. Massive change amplifies this problem even more. It puts all relationships in limbo until you get the time to evaluate each one. When I started my two-year journey, I did not reflect on this problem. I honestly wasn't aware of it. I felt overloaded with changes. I soon learned that I needed to be more aware of my surroundings and my feelings toward others. I tried to attempt to work on being 50 percent in all my relationships.

I know this sounds like I obliviously walked around with blinders on. I wasn't oblivious. I had reached a new level of personal growth. I became aware of things in finer details. Because of my new awareness, I started to figure out that not every friend is worth having a relationship—and some friends are just toxic. For those friends, they are only there for a limited time, and that is ok. The friendship was often based on some activity or common interest. After that activity or interest ends or exhausts itself, it is only natural for the relationship to fade away as you grow apart.

On the negative side, some relationships are just toxic. The relationship is not based on a 50/50 split. You might not even be aware of this toxicity until there is a change in the relationship or a light accidentally shines on it.

I am purposely not mentioning names in this chapter. I wish no ill will toward others, but I needed to cut the cords from quite a few people along my two-year journey. Also, just because my relationship with them was not 50/50, does not mean that they do not have relationships with other people that are 50/50. I had some relationships in my life that I became aware of as not being what they should be. One of them was toxic and the others didn't work out.

The first relationship that needed to end was one with a coworker, which was going to be a tricky one to extract myself out of. Normally if you have a person who is toxic in your life you can either let them know that you are no longer interested in having a relationship with them or just stop responding to their requests to do things together. Unfortunately, my toxic relationship was someone who I could not just cut out of my life. He was a coworker and his cubicle sat right next to mine. I still needed to work with this person, I just did not need to socialize with him or invest time in what he did.

This coworker was what I call an "energy vampire". Energy vampires are people with so much drama in their lives that they suck you in and feed off your goodwill toward them. They try to soak up as much of the air in a room as possible and suffocate you while leaving you exhausted. They want to be the center of attention and be acknowledged as special. They will do pretty much anything to maintain that view of themselves. You care for them and invest in their well being until they exhaust you to the point where you do not have the energy to do the things that make you happy.

My coworker, a hypochondriac, extracted emotional energy and channeled it toward himself. Time and time again this individual landed in the emergency room with different issues. It got so bad that for a time the emergency room tagged him as a drug abuser. His symptoms never added up to a conclusive diagnosis. He got prescribed medications for illnesses that he did not have. My coworker also had a lot of relationship problems. These problems just added to the drama he brought into the office.

I realized after a while that I had an energy vampire on my hands. I started to put some distance between myself and my coworker. I decided early on that having a conversation with him about his life and all the drama would just escalate the situation and invite even more drama and work issues. I did not want to be called into our Human Resources department for a meeting to ask me why I was being mean to a coworker. That never ends well for anyone.

What I decided to do after some thought on the subject was to build an "energy bubble" around me. For the sake of clarity, an energy bubble is one where I do not invest in the actions of the coworker or feel empathy toward him. I am a Reiki Master and I have never had to protect myself from anyone's bad energy, but this was a new day. I became increasingly aware of my changing mental and emotional state. I had the energy drained from me every work day, and it affected my home life.

I built a bubble around me while I worked—and to my surprise, I became aware of how much energy my coworker attempted to take from me. I found that when my coworker started telling stories that he told before, there were major inconsistencies in them. He told the stories to get people to feel sorry for him. Then he could ask favors and shift work to other people. It took a couple of weeks before my coworker realized that I was no longer a participant in his energy-sucking games. My coworker noticed the distance grow between us. I no longer showed interest in his health or relationship issues.

This shift led to some friction and his attempt to reset the relationship to bring me back into the fold. I decided that even though my coworker sat in the cubicle next to me, I would only talk to him about hospital business and nothing more. No health issues, no relationship issues, and I wouldn't get dragged into anything new with him. I also started stressing the good things that happened not just for me but for others we both knew. These good things included someone running their first marathon or a friend getting a new job. The stories were about other people. I stressed success and lack of failure. It brought a positive mood to the work environment. These positive events were being met by cynicism by my coworker.

The friction got greater and greater, and I stood my ground and did not drop my bubble. My coworker was clearly upset about the relationship change. It didn't work out for him. I started to make meetings during the lunch hour and schedule IT moves and changes to where there was no possibility of us having lunch. I wasn't being malicious—it was for my betterment. I was no longer going to be a part of emotionally charged drama.

It took my coworker about a month before he got another job. I believe he started looking for another job when he realized the new reality of our relationship. He went out the door a week later, and to my amazement, everything in the IT department started getting better. We have always been busy with projects, but more work got done and with fewer issues. This made my work environment much better. It also appeared that it made everyone's work relationships better. Cooperation between the different IT groups increased, and the stress level lowered for everyone.

I dropped my energy bubble at work once my coworker left. It enlightened me on friendships and what it meant being around a negative person. All you can be is 50 percent of a relationship, no more and no less for it to work in the long term. In the end, you can only do what is right for you, and the people around you either have to accept it or move on.

Energy vampires were not the only relationship issue I dealt with at this point in my journey. I had co-dependent problems—and this was my problem and only my problem. I so deeply wanted to help people achieve their goals that I was a co-dependence enabler. I enabled and encouraged behavior that made no sense in the long run. Yes, I participated in activities that helped others with their goals. I participated in their achievements. It was something that without me, they would not have the money to do on their own. The "without-me" part of that last sentence was the problem.

The common theme involved my co-dependent people living in the past. In a way, they were like the old me and wanted to regain their past capabilities. I spent a lot of money and time on activities where the person, who created the problem, got to participate, but when it came to my turn, there was always an issue. It took me a while to realize that I had a situation on my hands. In the end, I started to put some distance between myself and several of these people or groups of people. I made other plans and when asked to participate in their events, I would already be committed. I didn't take this approach to be mean or punish anyone. These relationships just weren't a good fit for me at the time.

If I am going to participate in an activity that I am paying for, I should be able to *participate* in it. That was the plan. This resulted in some friction between myself and my codependent people. Several of them called me a few times to complain that since I wasn't going to be at their events they could not do the event without me. Some attempted to use guilt to try and persuade me to participate. I shut those people down right away and ended my relationship with them. I do not do guilt.

Guilt is a nasty thing to attempt to put on others. This showed their true colors and what they thought of me. Guilt is a weapon that I do not have time for. Yes, some people got upset with me over my new priorities, but not all of them were bad people. I am still friends with some of these people, but I do not participate in their activities anymore. In the end, it has to be a good thing for me or a 50/50 relationship to work for the long term.

Massage school helped me deal with these people and the friction that it caused. This is good because just like my dealing with my coworker, I did not want to hurt people. I just needed an out to re-evaluate the relationship. I did not want to deal with codependency issues through direct confrontation. I have done that all my life, and it wasn't warranted here. I no longer made myself available on weekends. After massage class, I felt so tired that I did not want to go out. I also needed to spend time with my wife and my dog. Both missed me because I was out of the house a lot. I neglected the people who were closest to me, but they knew that there was a light at the end of the tunnel. Having to be in massage class for 500 hours to get my Certified Massage Therapy certificate saved me from my co-dependency problems. I looked at my relationships differently now. My two-year journey taught me that even good people can get wrapped up into something that does not end well.

There are more examples of people I grew apart from, but I want to concentrate on the positive changes. Looking back and asking the "why" question wastes time. Since everything changed around me, I honestly did not want to put on the brakes. If I was wrong about one of my codependent friends then I could always re-engage and tell them later what had been going on. If they are truly my friends they would understand.

The energy vampires, the co-dependent people, are out there—and you need to be aware of them. I am not suggesting to shun them or be angry with them. If the relationship isn't 50/50, it is a relationship that probably should be avoided. You can tell when you are around people like energy vampires or co-dependents—the draw is always to the other person. At no time does the energy vampire ever honestly become interested in what you do. It's all about them. With the co-dependents, you become aware of them when you aren't available or they want you to change your plans to help them do an activity that has financial and time cost involved. Their reactions are what needs to be observed. If it doesn't feel right, you might have a problem on your hands.

GRATITUDE AND GIVING

One of the things that surprised me the most on my two-year journey was how easy it was to show gratitude and give back to people. I discovered I enjoyed doing nice things for people. For example, I found it easy to take a little time and write a letter of recommendation for someone, so they could advance their careers or get hired in a job they really wanted. Also, the simple act of allowing others, by your decision, to go before you. This world is full of "Me-First" people. I found it refreshing to see the shock on people's faces when I would do something unexpected for a stranger. Don't get me wrong, there was a good reason for helping them, but I didn't do it to make myself look good. I wanted to make someone else's life a little better.

Simple acts of kindness are so easy to do if you think about it. It could be as simple as not taking your share of pizza when you aren't hungry and let others who are hungry, have it. You could take someone to lunch when things are financially or emotionally challenging for them. I found that once I got into massage school it became easy to be gracious and giving to my fellow school cohorts and friends.

Being older has its advantages in this process too. I have had people around me help me succeed. They opened the door for me to take ownership of my success. Charles "Butch" Stilson, my first bike coach, was a great example of this idea. He was a quadriplegic, but that did not take away from him assisting me. He used to get into my head to help me win my first bike race. Being a quadriplegic made him a better coach for me. It's amazing how he kept a super positive emotional state even with his challenges. This brings a different perspective to the idea that it can be easy to help someone, you just need to try.

I also felt more gratitude toward people. I am a Buddhist and in Buddhist teachings, it is not a mandate to give or help other people. Some may differ about that concept, but it is true to me. You need to want to help. It must be done with intention. This makes giving that much better—you do it for all the right reasons. I believe there is an "art" to giving (yes, I am playing a little game here, but my intention is worthy of the game). The art comes from the giving in a way that is well-accepted by the receiver and there is no requirement to repay the gift. It is like a gift with stealth qualities. The gift or help is laid out in front of the person who needs it—and it's accepted without guilt.

There are other things that come from gratitude. One, the social interaction between people who you have never met. These new-to-you friends could be found by doing simple things like hold a door open for someone who has his/her hands full; giving a couple of bucks to a mom who is attempting to buy some groceries and has come up a little short; or just having a smile on your face that makes it inviting for others to talk with you. You never know who you may run into, and each person has a story. Be interested in their stories and allow them the time and space to explore that story with you. Once you get them started telling you about their journeys, it is like a freight train coming at you. You learn a lot about them and it brings you closer to them. All it takes is to be open, have that nice and warm smile, and be present with them so they feel that you are interested in hearing what they have to say.

BUDDHISM

I was born into a family of members of the Episcopal Church or Church of England. I used to attend the St. Martin's Episcopal Church in Davis, Ca. When I was a little boy, I attended Sunday school every Sunday at St. Martins. I was even an alter boy in the church for a couple of years. I have to be honest, I never really liked going to church. I liked the subject matter. I liked the time spent at church, especially since I hadn't started racing bikes yet. I just had a problem with allowing myself to believe in God. I had developed a habit of passing out during the church services. I think God told me something back then: *I was destined to follow a different path.*

When I attended church services, I would get light-headed or hot and I just felt uncomfortable. I was an overactive kid with ADHD and dyslexia. I knew something was up when one Christmas service I sat in the front row right next to the altar and I passed out in the middle of the service. My family felt hugely embarrassed. I also scared the whole congregation that feared for my health. It ended my attending church services at St. Martins.

Once I hit junior high-school age I became an agnostic. I read a lot and self-reflected enough to decide to become agnostic. Mom and Dad didn't find the news good. I started traveling to race bikes over the weekends and found I didn't have time to go to church. I knew that if it was important to me later on in life I would follow up on my belief system.

As someone who has read the new and old testaments in ancient Greek, the Gnostic gospels found at Nag Hammadi and the Dead Sea scrolls, I would say that I am well-versed in early Christian faith. I used to talk with Mark about my beliefs when we would have a few cocktails after work. Now I didn't have Mark around to talk to anymore and I was unable to find anyone who could replace Mark in these conversations. I had to rely on my gut intuition to help me out in understanding my belief system and how it relates to the outside world.

I have historically been agnostic because I always considered myself pious. I know to most people this last statement makes no sense at all, but if you look at it from a pious standpoint, you cannot believe in something you cannot prove or disprove. I am personally doing the right thing by not believing in a higher being, regardless of what or who you call it. There is a leap of faith that goes on with all religion or your belief systems—and faith does not come easily to me.

Buddhism spoke to me because I am the higher power and I am striving to make myself better. This is what the two-year journey is all about. By bettering myself, I make the world a better place. The Buddhist world is one inside your own head where anything is possible. So, I am an accidental Buddhist because I stumbled onto Buddhism, which resonated with me and made perfect sense. I had been acting like a Buddhist for the last year or so. I just did not know it yet. I had become a much calmer person and much nicer to be around. I also do not like labels, so when the changes in my life happened, I didn't rush to put a label on it.

To me, it really did not need a label. It worked internally and in a lot of ways my life got easier. I felt more joyful, and it showed to others who cared to take a look. Since I do not feel religion should be worn on a sleeve so others can see, I am pretty quiet about being a Buddhist. I know that I am putting Buddhism in this book, but there is a good reason. It became a big part of all the changes that happened during my journey.

Religion is a personal choice. One person should never disparage someone for their religious beliefs. Under no circumstances should one push their religion on someone else. I see this happening a lot with people who just have found religion as a new convert or when someone is trying to convince you that they are the only true belief. When I see this happening, I waste no time discussing it with the person. I move away from them as quickly as possible. Personal belief is just that—personal.

Buddhism spoke to me, which is why I became a Buddhist. The tenants speak of the quietness of the mind, which was what I needed at the time. Buddhism for me is very simple. Yes, some people make it far more difficult than it needs to be, but I am taking the first Buddha's teachings and not going any further than that. Others who are on a different path, I am happy for them and I am just on my path. In my research that I have done over my two-year journey, I have found that just like Shinran Buddha, sometimes you need to leave what doesn't work for you and find out what does work for you. This becomes your new path, and you walk that path alone.

Below you will find the Four Noble Truths in my words and the Eightfold Path. The combination of these two simple concepts or rules governs me in my daily life. It amazes me it took me most of my life to find the answers I had been looking for and how much better my life became adopting the following:

The Four Noble Truths in my own words.
1. Suffering occurs
2. The cause of suffering is craving
3. The possibility for ending suffering exists
4. The cessation of suffering can be attained through the Eightfold Path

Eightfold Path
1. Right Understanding
2. Right Intention
3. Right Speech
4. Right Action
5. Right Livelihood
6. Right Effort
7. Right Mindfulness
8. Right Concentration

This simple listing of rules or concepts of Buddhism is pretty self-explanatory. I hope by reading this chapter you reflect on your situation and see what personally speaks to you. Whatever it is, make it yours and own it. You have a right to be one with your creator.

BOOKS

Reading became a big part of my two-year journey. I read with a purpose to help my journey. I figured if I stumbled on an idea of interest, there would be a book on the subject. I personally found and received recommendations on some really good books on all kinds of subjects. I did not do very much pleasure reading during this time, but I did stay pretty busy with the content learning on my reading list.

I have a long history of reading books with detailed content, but it wasn't always that way. I am dyslexic and learning impaired. I also have ADHD, but when I was younger and had a reading problem, they just called it hyperactive. As an elementary-school-age kid I had no idea about what it meant to be hyperactive. I was just being myself. I didn't learn how to read until the third grade. This had a devastating effect on me as a little kid. In class, when I wasn't in special education classes, if someone laughed at me for not reading or mixing up math problems, I full force went at them. I would see red and attack. I developed some terrible behavioral problems. I needed help and sadly some understanding. I chronically claimed it wasn't fair. I asked, "Why is this happening to me?" I couldn't see the big picture at such a young age.

Help for me came in the form of my mother driving me twice a week to Orinda, Ca for reading lessons. This was not a short drive from Davis, Ca. They had a special reading school that helped people like me. It took a couple of years to accomplish but I finally obtained the ability to read at grade level through working with the school in Orinda and reading at night with my mom. To this day, the only person who can call me "Scotty" is my reading instructor in Orinda. She has a special place in my heart.

Now that I could read on my own, I felt very proud. I did not realize at the time what amount of effort went into all those trips to the school in Orinda and how it helped me succeed. This also had a side effect on me that no one saw coming. I have always been negatively motivated or reinforced. I am not saying I was abused, far from it. The people who reached me were the ones who simply said I could not do something—and then I went about proving them wrong. I think this is where my competitive streak comes from.

A side effect of learning to read made me aware and scared that I would lose the ability to read. This fear wasn't rational. It was a real fear for someone in the third grade. I now felt motivated to never lose the ability to read, so I never stopped reading. Once I could read, I dove in. Political philosophy and conceptual science attracted me. Later on, I acquired the love of reading history and learning topics that came up and interested me. This two-year journey was full of books that if I was not on this journey, I would have never read. Below are the books that stood out as meaningful for me over my journey.

The Spark In The Machine

The first book, a massage- and energy-related book, was recommended by one of my instructors, Kathleen. Kathleen specializes in Acupressure and Reflexology. She had a teaching style that resonated with me. In September 2017, I had recently taken my first acupressure class from Kathleen, which came right after my hospital stay for AFIB. The class was Acupressure for Neck and Shoulders. Her book suggestion came in an email. I reached out to her because I wanted to know how energy moves through the body and how the body develops. This book spoke directly to both of those subjects in a way I could understand it. I always enjoyed being in Kathleen's classroom, and I took many classes from her. When she suggested the book, I did not hesitate to purchase and start reading it. I needed more base knowledge before I could understand the finer details of the subjects. This book fit perfectly with where I was knowledge wise.

The book *The Spark in the Machine* by Dr. Daniel Keown contained a lot answers for me, along with a longer list of new questions. It is strange how that happens to me all the time. This book dealt with the way energy moves through the body. It also takes a very close look at how the evolution of the embryo to birth of the newborn and develops along those energy lines. Those energy lines eventually become your meridians. The more I studied massage, the more I became interested in traditional Chinese medicine (TCM) and those energy meridian lines. There was so much content in this book that I read it twice before reporting back to Kathleen that I had finished it. This book laid the foundation for my work with acupressure since I am not licensed to use needles. It is probably better that way. I do not have the steadiest hands because of the hyperthyroidism I developed when I was 34-years old. Sticking someone with needles kind of requires steady hands.

Stealing Fire

The next book was a recommendation from Karlie, one of my massage cohorts from Massage Fundamentals. Karlie was so impressed with the book that she insisted that I check it out. We were at a Mexican Restaurant in Davis, Ca at the time. I bought the book online while we were eating dinner. The book titled *Stealing Fire* by Steven Kotler and Jamie Wheal conveys the concept of how different groups of people use something called "flow" to overcome obstacles and perform at an elevated level. I already knew about the flow they were talking about. There were many instances when I bike raced with my teammates where I could execute a move without talking to them. This non-verbal communication happened at a higher level of understanding. It just happens in the right situation. If you have to think about it, it is too late, you missed your opportunity to execute. In the book, the authors talk with Silicon Valley Executives and Navy Seals. The Navy Seals have to use flow to get things done. They have to know what to do instinctively and by muscle memory. They have to move with precision and in silence. They practice for what they are going to do and execute on what they practice.

Silicon Valley executives also have a type of flow. The executives have to make decisions in the now and cannot just "wait" to make decisions. Their decisions equate to millions or billions of dollars, and they have to be sure and committed to their actions.

I didn't agree with everything in the book. The authors love affair with "Burning Man" is not something I share, but they do make a compelling argument about community of thought and flow.

The take-away from *Stealing Fire* is the book provided an opening into flow meditations. I purchased their ear sensor from Heart Labs and software that got installed on my cell phone. You need the earpiece and the software to participate with their flow-meditation program. The objective in flow meditation is to use the ear sensor to meditate in a way that gives you a certain type of heart rhythm. This way, if your heart rhythm is correct for flow, the app will make a positive sound and a green circle shows at the top of the cell phone app. I did this for a short time. Then I got interested in another type of meditation. There is nothing wrong with flow meditation. Look at others who do flow meditation. They receive a lot of benefit from doing it.

I decided to discontinue from using the device and application because of the next book. I wanted to take my meditating in a different direction. I did not want my cell phone around while I meditated. I also thought the beeping of the app caused distraction, but even with the sound turned off, I still felt distracted by the phone.

The Mind Illuminated

The Mind Illuminated has been mentioned in this book in the Mindfulness chapter. *The Mind Illuminated* was suggested by my mindfulness instructor, Per. *The Mind Illuminated* by John Yates sat on my Kindle for a while before I read it. I have to admit that this book intimidated me a bit. The idea that there are many levels in meditation confused me at first. A lot of what I believed was simply wrong.

Once I started reading the book, I overcame all reading and understanding obstacles. With each of the previous books that I read, I did for a specific reason. I tried to address these issues, and *The Mind Illuminated* was more of a roadmap for me. I had started a meditation practice that I attempted to do every day. *The Mind Illuminated* gave me a way to chart my progress in meditation and an understanding of what happened to me and why. The book explained what to expect on each level of meditations. I found the book spoke to me in simple terms. It was a work in progress for me to continue to improve my meditation.

CONCLUSION

The end of my journey came on January 1, 2019. I wanted the last thing to be to meet with Nancy and discuss what I had learned along my journey. The reason for doing this was simple: I wanted to put closure on the journey. Nancy took me over the finish line. There turned out to be a few takeaways from my journey and some surprised me.

The first thing is that I am really happy that I took the challenge and trusted myself to take the journey in the first place. The overcoming of the resistance to change was bigger than I thought when I started. This was a very big step, and it came off a big loss in my life with the death of my good friend Mark.

During the journey I have asked myself the obvious question, and that is, would I have done the journey even without the loss? The answer is yes. I would have participated in the journey, but it would have taken longer and it would not have been so impactful on me. This journey has fundamentally changed my life forever. I look at the journey as all things happen for a reason, and it is how you react to it that is important.

The second thing involved working with my three therapists, which turned out to be the smartest thing I could have ever done. Now I know the way I went about things was a bit different. It should be different from how others do it. It was my solution and what I needed at the time. I trusted the process of letting go and allowing the universe to steer for a while. I really trusted my therapists—and that is the most important part of therapy. If you are afraid or not willing to go deep into the most terrible places in your mind with your therapist then this person is not right for you. Do not accept the middle-of-the-road therapists; you will spend more time and money with them and may not get the resolution you look for.

The one thing that surprised me most about the whole journey was how I needed to work on the small things first. If the small things fell into place to create big change, the large issues just took care of themselves. Therapy helped me that way, but it became a stepping stone to what I think was the linchpin of the whole journey—and that was finding massage school.

So many things happened around the time period of massage school. I figured out who were my good friends and who were not. I realized that my cell phone had become the enemy of my marriage and any close relationships. I adapted mindfulness and became a Buddhist. I got a good handle on volunteering and actually making a difference in other people's lives. I learned, accepted, and practiced gratitude. I found a group of special people to do my massage fundamentals. These bonds became very tight. They helped me feel welcome and confident enough to get out there and welcome others. I think that part was a major step in the right direction. I no longer competed with everyone else. I joined them in a common effort to make this world a little better, one person at a time. I also saw this as working on the small things that became big things of change. If I could help someone feel so good about what they do then move on and work with someone else—big things are bound to happen.

In the end, I am going to go back to my philosophy days in college and borrow a quote that was one of my first quotes to touch me deeply.

"A life not examined, is a life not worth living."
- Socrates

I started this journey with a quote from T.S Lawrence about being a daydreamer willing to dare to dream during the day to a quote from Socrates about examining one's life. I think this is the best explanation of how an ego-driven, self-centered athlete can change into a Buddhist, a Reiki Master, and a certified massage therapist who works to help others get a glimpse of their athletic or personal capabilities.

This leads me to say:

"Think and therefore you shall do and dare to dream in the day and act on that dream. The day will come where you will examine your life and accept who and what you are and what you will become in the future, if you accept the challenge."
- Scott Spiess

AND WHAT IS NEXT FOR SCOTT?

The journey is over, so what is next for Scott? That is a great question and one that I thought about a lot between my last massage class and the meeting with Nancy on January 1, 2019. Throughout the journey, I felt like I was doing and discovering things so quickly that I was not getting a good depth with the different subject matters. During the journey, I decided that it would be a shame to just gloss over the different subjects, but I also could not stop the discovery train to accommodate my desire to know more about different subjects I had been exposed to. There were just too many things happening at one time to even prioritize.

To deal with this issue, I did what I did at the start of the journey. I let go and discovered as much as I could with no stress, knowing I could always go back. I made this promise in the book with Reiki and NLP otherwise known as Neurolistic Programing. So, it makes perfect sense to take the subjects that resonated with me and do a deep-dive, post-two-year journey.

I have listed a few of the subjects that I took up and what my findings were.

It all started with Reiki. Reiki helped me help Mark for the limited time he had left on the face of the planet. I made a promise that if I continued with Reiki, I would get the proper schooling around the traditional route to Reiki Master. In late June 2019, I started back on the path to Reiki Master through a local Reiki Master who is well-respected in my area. Marion has helped to refresh my memory on what I learned so quickly back at the start of my journey.

I started classes again from Reiki One through a Reiki Master who knows the actual teaching of Reiki. I got with five other Reiki students to go through the master's program together. We all have different stories—and we all love Reiki. Working as a group we have all gotten stronger with our capabilities and the energy that we create. Every class is like a Reiki share, where we all work on each other. By the time this book is published I should have earned the status of Reiki Master—that is, in the traditional way.

Therapy

I am no longer seeking any type of therapy. I will not hesitate to start again if I feel the need, but my therapeutic effort on the two-year journey puts an end to my need to seek help. I have a very stable home life, with two good jobs. I will get to the second job later. I also have a lot of learning that is going on that has the side effect of making me feel very content. I have said for a long time that seeking happiness is not the most productive way of being happy with one's self. Seeking contentment allows happiness to thrive with no effort in producing it.

Massage School

Massage school was the most motivational change mover during my journey. I met so many interesting people with whom I am still in touch with to this day. Sofi and Reece, who were part of my massage fundamentals class, helped with this book as I interviewed both of them while I wrote the book.

I continue to take massage classes as I have time. I still have an interest in acupressure and structural integration.

I have branched out in the massage world, and I have been hired to be the Massage Therapist at the Roseville, Ca campus for Hewlett Packard. I am not an HP employee; I am a contractor, but they have quite a few cyclists and distance runners for me to work with.

AFIB

In August 2019 I underwent a heart procedure called an Ablation. It is too early to tell yet if the ablation will take or not, but I have a 70 percent chance of it being corrected. I think positive thoughts about it. I hope I never come down with another case of AFIB for the rest of my life. I am so looking forward to not taking those prescription medications.

Volunteering

I am still actively volunteering at different events with massage groups. I have signed up for 10 events in 2019. I will continue to work with them in future years. Since I have been able to work with the ultramarathon runners for a couple of years now, I am further working with them on the mental game of endurance sports. Most of the work is done while I have them on my massage table at the events and my help centers around defeating self-doubt in endurance events.

I am actively looking for other great organizations to volunteer with to help people realize what their capabilities can be.

10 QUICK TIPS

Top 10 tips to help you with change:

1. Make the decision to change and do not look back or second-guess yourself.
2. Do not be hard on yourself; there will be trips and falls.
3. Do not sweat the small stuff—in the end, it does not matter.
4. Love yourself first because no one can love you if you do not love yourself.
5. Do not worry if you are right or wrong, it is the journey that is important.
6. Do not let guilt in your life; it is an emotion that helps no one.
7. Please understand no one achieves perfection on the first day.
8. You are your best subject matter expert on yourself.
9. Forgiveness is for you, not the other person.
10. Do not try and control things, those things will end up controlling you.

AN HONEST THANK YOU

I would like to take the time and thank you for following me along this two-year journey. It has been an interesting time with all that I have learned and experienced. I have made life-long friendships with many people over this journey. I was able to become a better person because of it. I have to admit that the journey was tough, but coming out the other side has made me a more patient and giving person. I really love helping people with massage and having a close and honest conversation with them. This is a gift that I give to myself and anyone else who happens to spark up a conversation with me.

I value being present with people and learning who they really are. I do not focus on things like job title or what they do. Most of the people I run into have something special going on in their lives that they value more than working or scaling that corporate ladder. I see people seeing value in an experience, instead of watching it on a video. Being present is a very valuable thing, and it is a lesson I learned on this journey.

I hope after you finish reading this book, you reflect on how you can have a two-year journey of your own. Who knows, you just might change yourself, become happier, and learn a few things about yourself.

ACKNOWLEDGMENTS

I want to take this time to acknowledge the people who helped me write this book. I would like to thank my mother and father whose support throughout the years has given me the confidence to put a pencil to paper and write this book. I would also like to thank my wife Sandra Spiess, my brother Craig Spiess, and my sister Nora Grabar. They gave me moral support when I was questioning myself about my story and if it was worth reading.

I would like to thank my draft readers and editors for helping me get this book into a flowing story. I could not have done it without you. To my readers, Nora Grabar, Kelly Hartigan, and Sandra Spiess—thank you for giving me your time. Time is the most valuable thing we have and I valued your efforts to get this book written.

To Michelle Gamble, I know how much effort you put into making this book happen. I truly appreciate it and I hope we both can look at this effort as a success. I know we both have a passion for helping people and we both look to inspire others to overcome their resistance to change.

To my therapists, I hope this book has done you all justice. To Samantha Hudson Geiger, you are my 12-pound sledgehammer to the side of my head. I appreciate your style and the willingness to get in the trenches with me. Your process worked.

To Lynn Kennedy Baxter, I really made progress with you and I hope you realize it. You were the right person for me at the time. I valued my time with you.

To Nancy Georges, thanks for being out of the box with me—your personal strength kept me moving forward. We crossed the finish line together at the end of my two-year journey. You were the right person to finish the two-year journey with.

To my massage instructors, I do not know if you are aware of how much you helped in this journey. Each one of you impacted me in a special way. You reached me. You helped a very rigid person with very little feelings to one who now helps people with skills acquired in your classroom. I hope I make you proud.

Jim Burns, thanks for working with me and showing me what dedication is in Ortho-Bionomy. You helped me get comfortable working on others with confidence.

Kathleen Davis, you have inspired me to look further and further into traditional Chinese Medicine. Your Acupressure and Reflexology classes got me thinking about solving problems in different ways. These classes and your friendship have led me to be a life-long learner—and that desire continues to this day.

Jim Gilkeson, you opened my eyes to energy work and calmness. Your classes were always eye opening and left me with an idea that I could do anything in energy work.

Sharon Oshita, you were my all-around wonder. Your classes filled in the holes in my knowledge gap in working with people with injuries. I also loved the way you kept me in line. Since I work with a lot of athletes, I used what you taught me on a daily basis and I thank you for showing interest in me.

To my fellow massage students, if you worked with me in class, I truly thank you for your patience, willingness to work with the old guy, and your love and compassion. I want to single out a few people who were especially impactful. Alma Pham, Sofi Rubio, Reece Love, and Karli Olson, you guys/gals simply are the best and no one could ask for better classmates. You all saw me stumble with techniques and fall down, but you still worked with me to polish up my massage skills. I love that you saw the change in me as it was happening and not only embraced it but also helped move it along. You accepted my awkwardness in the beginning and you embraced me as a friend. I could not have had better classmates. With love and respect to you all.

I want to acknowledge two people who will never read this. First to my first bike racing coach Charles "Butch" Stilson. I do not think you ever realized what you did for me. You helped me in the most significant moment of my life, my first win. You were my second Dad and you came into my life at the right time to help me succeed at a dream. We accomplished that dream.

To Mark Miller, you made this book happen. Without you, I would have had problems overcoming my resistance to change. Unfortunately, you never were able to see the fruits of your labor. Your friendship with me was special and there was a very strong bond between us. I cannot watch a Formula One race without thinking about you. You are greatly missed and cannot be replaced—go with peace my friend.

Last but not least I would like to thank the people who read this book. I hope this book helps you along your journey to organic change. Pushing past the line of resistance to change is not an easy thing to do. I hope you take a few ideas from the book and push forward. There is no static roadmap to change. You just need to understand that you need to find your path and take that first step. I applaud you for your efforts and do not be too tough on yourself. There will be some tripping and falling along the way. To win you have to finish the race. Take your time; no one has a stopwatch in his or her hands. It is up to you.

ABOUT THE AUTHOR

Scott Spiess has a master's degree in information systems along with a bachelor's degree in Social Science and a minor in Philosophy. Scott through his two-year journey has earned the certification of Reiki Master and Certified Massage Therapist. Scott has been a member of the United States National Cycling Team and represented his country in the Jr. World Championships in Mery Corbon, France in 1984, along with several national tours. Scott has worked diligently with his clients to increase their abilities to succeed at anything they put their minds to doing. Scott has overcome many life and health issues to continue pushing forward with a positive attitude that inspires others. For more information, visit my website at scottspiess.com.